ISBN 978-2-7005-0764-5
ISSN 2266-1158
Graphic design: Atwazart

Korean

Inseon Kim

Adapted for English speakers by
Beomjoon Park

B.P. 25
94431 Chennevières sur Marne cedex
France

This phrasebook doesn't claim to be a substitute for a language course, but if you devote a bit of time to reading it and learning a few useful phrases, you'll quickly find that you're able to participate in basic exchanges with Korean speakers, enriching your travel experience.

A word of advice: don't aim for perfection! Those you're speaking to will forgive any mistakes and appreciate your efforts to communicate in their language. The main thing is to leave your inhibitions behind and speak!

Section I

INTRODUCTION 9

Section II

GETTING STARTED 15

Section III

CONVERSING 57

Section IV

Introduction

How to use this book

Section 1: Getting started in Korean

Can you spare a half an hour a day? Do you have three weeks ahead of you before your trip? In that case, jump in with the mini-lessons specially designed to familiarize you with Korean in just 21 days. These mini-lessons are aimed at beginners with no prior knowledge of Korean and will give you the basics you need to understand and address people in all sorts of situations.

• Discover the day's lesson, using the official Romanization transliterations of the Korean characters (supported by our phonetic transcriptions) to read the Korean out loud.
• Check the translation in everyday English, as well as the word-for-word translation, which will help you get used to the structure of the language.
• Read the notes that follow the lesson – these explain key linguistic points so you can apply them in other contexts.
• Finally, do the short exercise to consolidate what you've learned.

The next day, move on to the following lesson! Taking the time to do a little Korean each day is the most effective way to learn it.

Section 2: Conversing

This section gives you the tools you'll need for dealing with a variety of situations during your trip. It provides useful vocabulary and expressions that you can use in a range of contexts. The Korean phrases are accompanied by their Romanized equivalents, as well as phonetic transcriptions for help with pronunciation. This ready-to-use 'survival kit' is all you need to be an independent traveller!

South Korea: facts & figures

This guide focuses on South Korea.

Surface area	100,210 km²
Population	50 million
Capital	Seoul 서울 (pop. 10 million)
Nearest neighbours	North Korea, Japan, China
Sea boundaries	East China Sea, Yellow Sea, East Sea (Sea of Japan)
Official language	Korean (한국어 **hangugeo** *[han-goo-gaw]*)
Currency	won 원 (₩, KRW)
Government	Democratic republic
National holiday	15 August (National Liberation Day)
Main religions	Protestantism, Catholicism and Buddhism

A bit of history

'Land of the Morning Calm'

In the West, Korea is known as the 'Land of the Morning Calm', which derives from a British painter's poetic translation of the name of the Joseon dynasty (1392–1910), the last imperial dynasty to rule Korea (**joseon** *[cho-sawn]* literally means 'morning brightness'). Fortuitously, the name also reflects Korean philosophy, which is based on Confucianism. The central doctrine of the Joseon dynasty (the previous dynasties were Buddhist), Confucianism is a set of teachings and ethical values that transmit a world view and a way of life. The ideal Confucian is 'a person of virtue', i.e. someone who is humane, kind, honest, respectful, modest and loyal.

A dynamic, modern country

Since it became independent after World War II, South Korea has experienced spectacular growth – today it has the 13th largest economy in the world. A number of its multinationals have become household names (Samsung, LG, Hyundai, Kia, etc.). A Korean form of family-controlled corporate group is the **chaebol** *[cheh-bohl]*; these have played a key role in developing industry. In recent years, Korea has also had impressive success with its cultural exports, from K-pop and K-dramas to film, fashion and food – a trend known as 한류 **hallyu** *[hal-yoo]* *the Korean Wave*.

The Korean language

Korean is considered to be in a distinct Koreanic language family, although grammatically there is similarity between Korean and Japanese, and some of its vocabulary comes from Chinese.

Originally, Korean was written using Chinese characters, a writing system that lasted over 1000 years. In 1443, King Sejong the Great commissioned an alphabet that would be both more adapted to writing Korean and simpler to learn. His aim was to increase literacy by making reading and writing easier for common people. This alphabet, today known in South Korea as **Hangeul** 한글 *[han-guhl]* ('Korean script') and in North Korea as **Joseonmal** 조선말 *[cho-sawn-mal]* ('Korea speech'), was made official in both North and South Korea after World War II. (The separation between these nations in the intervening years has led to certain differences in pronunciation and vocabulary.)

This guide gives the Romanized equivalents of **Hangeul** (or **Hangul** in the former system). These are based on the Revised Romanization officially adopted in South Korea in 2000. For example, in this system, Samsung would be 'Samseong' and Hyundai 'Hyeondae'.

The alphabet

The Korean alphabet has 14 basic consonants and 10 basic vowels as well as 5 double consonants and 11 double vowels.

Basic consonants*

ㄱ **g** or **k**	ㄴ **n**	ㄷ **d** or **t**	ㄹ **r** or **l**	ㅁ **m**	ㅂ **b** or **p**	ㅅ **s** or **t**	ㅇ - or **ng**
ㅈ **j** or **t**	ㅊ **ch** or **t**	ㅋ **k**	ㅌ **t**	ㅍ **p**	ㅎ **h** or **t**		

*A number of the consonants are pronounced differently depending on the sound that occurs before or after them. See the front cover flap.

Basic vowels

ㅏ **a**	ㅑ **ya**	ㅓ **eo**	ㅕ **yeo**	ㅗ **o**	ㅛ **yo**	ㅜ **u**	ㅠ **yu**
ㅡ **eu**	ㅣ **i**						

Double consonants

These are pronounced more strongly than single consonants.

ㄲ **kk** or **k**	ㄸ **tt**	ㅃ **pp**	ㅆ **ss** or **t**	ㅉ **jj**

Double vowels

These are formed by combining the basic vowels. Spoken quickly, the sounds blend together as diphthongs.

ㅐ **ae**	ㅒ **yae**	ㅔ **e**	ㅖ **ye**	ㅘ **wa**	ㅙ **wae**	ㅚ **oe**	ㅝ **wo**
ㅞ **we**	ㅟ **wi**	ㅢ **ui**					

The shapes of the consonants ㄱ **g/k**, ㄴ **n**, ㅁ **m**, ㅅ **s/t** and ㅇ **ng** are representations of the shape the speech organs make to pronounce them. The other consonants are based on these shapes, but with additional lines. Korean vowels are one or a combination of three linear strokes. These represent elements of the universe (the heavens are symbolized by a short horizontal line '-', the earth by a long horizontal line '—', and a human being by a vertical line ' | ').

A syllabic language

In Korean, the characters in the alphabet are combined in the form of 'blocks' to represent syllables. So when you see a symbol in Korean writing, it is actually composed of separate characters, and the entire block corresponds to a specific syllable. All syllable blocks consist of at least one consonant followed by a vowel. Some also have a final consonant. Essentially, the characters in the alphabet are used as building blocks to make composite symbols that always start with a consonant, then add a vowel, and possibly end with a final consonant. For example, the symbol 글 **geul** *[guhl] script, writing* is made up of the character ㄱ **g** (top), — **eu** (middle) and ㄹ **l** (bottom). (Note: If the vowel is a long vertical stroke, it is placed to the right of the initial consonant; if it is a horizontal line, it is placed below the initial consonant.)

Pronunciation

In this phrasebook, words and expressions are given in **Hangeul** accompanied by the Romanization and a phonetic transcription. The hyphens in the latter separate the syllable blocks, but when spoken the sounds run together (in the phonetic transcriptions, some syllables don't start with a consonant–this means the first consonant is silent). The front cover flap has a pronunciation key to help you correctly pronounce the different sounds in Korean.

Once you're familiar with the alphabet, you'll have the basic tools to pronounce each consonant and vowel within a syllable block.

However, one of the trickiest aspects for learners is that many Korean consonants have several different pronunciations depending on adjacent sounds.

• Some consonants change sound according to their location in a syllable (i.e. if it is the initial, medial or final sound). Examples include the consonants ㄱ, ㄷ, ㅂ and ㄹ, which are pronounced as **g**, **d**, **b** and **r** when followed by a vowel, but as **k**, **t**, **p** and **l** when followed by another consonant or at the end of a word. Another example is the character ㅎ, which can change the pronunciation of the consonant before or after it: so in the word 어떻게 **eotteoke** *[aw-Taw-kay]* *by what means, how*, the ㅎ at the end of the second syllable turns the following ㄱ into a **k**. Additionally, some consonants in the final position are barely pronounced – we indicate this by putting it in superscript.

• There is also a set of consonants that have three different forms with three different pronunciations: 'plain' or unaspirated consonants (ㄱ **g**, ㄷ **d**, ㅂ **b**, ㅅ **s** and ㅈ **j**), 'aspirated' consonants (i.e. pronounced by forcefully expelling air) (ㅋ **k**, ㅌ **t**, ㅍ **p** and ㅊ **ch**) or 'tense' (stressed) consonants (ㄲ **kk**, ㄸ **tt**, ㅃ **pp**, ㅆ **ss** and ㅉ **jj**). These double consonants are pronounced like the single equivalents, but more strongly.

In any case, don't let these variations intimidate you – the phonetic transcriptions indicate how a consonant should be pronounced in the context where it appears.

So now you're ready to get started! 행운을 빌어요 **haenguneul bireoyo!** *[heng-oon-uhl peer-aw-yo]* *Good luck!*

Getting started

Day 1

어디예요? eodiyeyo?
Where is it?

1 어디예요?
eodi·yeyo?
where-be
Where are [you]?

2 한국이에요.
hangug·ieyo.
Korea-be
[I] am [in] Korea.

3 누구예요?
nugu·yeyo?
who-be
Who are [you]?

4 캐롤이에요.
kaeror·ieyo.
Carol-be
[I] am Carol.

5 무엇이에요?
mueos·ieyo?
what-be
What is [it]?

6 여권이에요.
yeogwon·ieyo.
passport-be
[It] is [a] passport.

***1** aw-dee-yay-yo **2** han-gook-ee-ay-yo **3** noo-goo-yay-yo **4** keh-rol-ee-ay-yo **5** moo-awsh-ee-ay-yo **6** yaw-kwon-ee-ay-yo*

Notes

In the Romanization in the lessons, we use dots to separate suffixes to help you identify the different parts of the word. In the phonetic transcriptions under the dialogue, we use hyphens to separate each syllable (which corresponds to a Korean syllable block). But keep in mind that the syllables blend together when spoken quickly.

The subject in a Korean sentence is very often omitted as the context usually makes it clear who or what the verb refers to. The subject is expressed only when really necessary.

The verb is always placed at the end of a sentence. Verbs do not conjugate according to person – good news! However, there are three forms depending on the degree of politeness required: colloquial (for friends or peers), polite informal and polite formal. We have opted for the polite informal, which means a sentence always ends with 요 -**yo**. This is the most frequently used form, both in speech and writing. It is a polite way to address someone you don't know well (Koreans also use it to address people who are older than them, normally including their parents).

To form a question, just use a rising intonation.

이에요 **ieyo** *[ee-ay-yo]* / 예요 **yeyo** *[yay-yo]* correspond to the verb *to be*. After a word that ends with a consonant, 이에요 **ieyo** is used. After a word that ends with a vowel, 예요 **yeyo** is used. There is no real difference in pronunciation. Note that there is no space between *be* and the word preceding it.

Practice – Translate the following sentences:

1. What is it?
2. Who are you?
3. 어디예요?
4. 여권이에요.

Answers:

1. 무엇이에요?
2. 누구예요?
3. Where are you?
4. It's a passport.

Day 2

한국에 가요 **hanguge gayo**
I'm going to Korea

1 어디에 가요?
eodi·e gayo?
where-[destination] go
Where are you going?

2 한국에 가요.
hangug·e gayo.
Korea-[destination] go
I'm going to Korea.

3 언제 한국에 가요?
eonje hangug·e gayo?
when Korea-[destination] go
When are you going to Korea?

4 캐나다에서 와요?
kaenada·eseo wayo?
Canada-[place-of-origin] come
Do you come from Canada?

5 아니요. 미국에서 와요.
aniyo. migug·eseo wayo.
no. United-States-[place-of-origin] come
No, I come from the United States.

1 *aw-dee-ay ka-yo* ***2*** *han-gook-ay ka-yo* ***3*** *awn-jay han-gook-ay ka-yo*
4 *keh-na-da-ay-saw wa-yo* ***5*** *ah-nee-yo mee-gook-ay-saw wa-yo*

Notes

Korean nouns are very simple to use. There is no definite article (*the*) or indefinite article (*a, an, some*), and typically the same form is used for the singular and plural, except if the speaker wants to emphasize that there is more than one of something. So the subject pronouns (*I, you, he, she, we, they*) are rarely used, verbs don't conjugate for person, and nouns typically have just one form–easier than you thought, isn't it?

One main difference from English is that Korean uses grammatical particles to indicate the function of a noun in the sentence (subject, object, place, time, etc.). The particle is attached as a suffix to the end of the noun. This dialogue has two particles that indicate location: the particle 에 **-e** *[ay]* indicates destination (*to*). The particle 에서 **-eseo** *[ay-saw]* indicates a departure point or place of origin (*from*).

Practice–Translate the following sentences:

1. Where are you going?
2. Where do you come from? / Where are you coming from?
3. 미국에서 와요.
4. 한국에 가요.

Answers:

1. 어디에 가요?
2. 어디에서 와요?
3. I come from the United States.
4. I'm going to Korea.

Day 3

비빔밥을 먹어요 bibimbabeul meogeoyo
I eat bibimbap

1 식당에서 비빔밥을 먹어요.
sikdang·eseo bibimbab·eul meogeoyo.
restaurant-[place-of-action] bibimbap-[object] eat
[I'm] eating bibimbap at the restaurant.

2 슈퍼에서 음료수를 사요.
syupeo·eseo eumnyosu·reul sayo.
supermarket-[place-of-action] drink-[object] buy
[I'm] buying a drink at the supermarket.

3 무엇을 해요?
mueos·eul haeyo?
what-[object] do
What are [you] doing?

4 친구를 만나요.
chingu·reul mannayo.
friend-[object] meet
[I'm] meeting my friends.

***1** shi[k]-tahng-ay-saw pee-bim-pap-uhl mawg-aw-yo **2** shoo-paw-ay-saw um-nyo-soo-ruhl sa-yo **3** moo-aws-uhl-heh-yo **4** chin-goo-ruhl man-na-yo*

Notes

The particles 을 **-eul** *[uhl]* / 를 **-reul** *[ruhl]* are used to indicate a direct object (what directly receives the action of the verb). If the direct object ends with a consonant, the suffix 을 **-eul** is added, and if it ends with a vowel, 를 **-reul** is added. This particle is very often omitted in spoken language.

As we saw in the previous lesson, the location particle 에서 **eseo** *[ay-saw]* is used to indicate place of origin or a departure point. It also indicates the location of an action – this is the way it is used in lines 1 and 2. Note that the present tense in Korean can sometimes translate to the English present continuous: e.g. 먹어요 **meogeoyo** *[mawg-aw-yo]* *I eat, I am eating, you eat, you are eating*, etc.

The suffixes can make Korean words seem long, but once you get used to identifying the particles, the base words are not so intimidating: e.g. 식당 **sikdang** *[shik-tahng]* *restaurant*, 무엇 **mueot** *[moo-aw^t]* *what, something*, 친구 **chingu** *[chin-goo]* *friend*, etc.

Practice – Translate the following sentences:

1. I go to the restaurant.
2. I eat at the restaurant.
3. 식당에서 비빔밥을 먹어요.
4. 식당에서 와요.

Answers:

1. 식당에 가요.
2. 식당에서 먹어요.
3. I'm eating bibimbap at the restaurant.
4. I'm coming from the restaurant.

Day 4

지하철역이 어디에 있어요?
jihacheolyeogi eodie isseoyo
Where is the metro station?

1 지하철역이 어디에 있어요?
jihacheolyeog·i eodi·e isseoyo?
metro-station-[subject] where-[place] exist
Where is the metro station?

2 저기에 있어요.
jeogi·e isseoyo.
over-there-[place] exist
It's over there.

3 기차역이 있어요?
gichayeog·i isseoyo?
train-station-[subject] exist
Is there a train station?

4 기차가 언제 와요?
gicha·ga eonje wayo?
train-[subject] when arrive
When does the train arrive?

5 근처에 택시가 있어요?
geuncheo·e taeksi·ga isseoyo?
nearby-[place] taxi-[subject] exist
Is there a place to catch a taxi nearby?

***1** chee-a-chawl-yawk-ee aw-dee-ay eess-aw-yo **2** chaw-kee-ay eess-aw-yo **3** kee-cha-yawk-ee eess-aw-yo **4** kee-cha-ga awn-jay wa-yo **5** kuhn-chaw-ay tek-shee-ga eess-aw-yo*

Notes

The compound word 지하철역 **jihacheolyeog** *[chee-a-chawl-yaw*k*]* *metro station* is made up of 지하철 **jihacheol** *[chee-a-chawl]* *metro* + 역 **yeog** *[yaw*k*]* *station*.

The particles 이 **-i** *[ee]* / 가 **-ga** *[ga]* are used to indicate the subject of the verb. The suffix 이 **-i** is used if the noun ends with a consonant; 가 **-ga** is used if it ends with a vowel.

We've seen that the location particle 에 **-e** *[ay]* indicates destination (see Day 2). It is also used to indicate a location with the verb 있어요 **isseoyo** *[eess-aw-yo]*, meaning *to be (located) somewhere*: e.g. 어디에 있어요? *Where is it?* 저기에 있어요. *It's over there.* 기차에 있어요. *It's in the train*.

The verb 있어요 **isseoyo** literally means *to exist* (among other things), but often translates to *there is/are* in English: 기차가 있어요. **gichaga isseoyo.** *There's a train.* ('train-[subject] exists'). Word order in Korean is not rigid (except for the verb, which is always placed at the end of sentence). As long as the particle indicates the subject's function, it can be placed anywhere in the sentence. However, it is usually the first word.

Practice – Translate the following sentences:

1. There is a metro station nearby.
2. Where is the train station?
3. 저기에 택시가 있어요.
4. 기차가 언제 와요?

Answers:

1. 근처에 지하철역이 있어요. **2.** 기차역이 어디에 있어요?
3. There's a taxi over there. **4.** When does the train arrive?

Day 5

저는 한국 친구가 있어요
jeoneun hanguk chinguga isseoyo
I have Korean friends

1 제롬 씨는 외국 친구가 있어요?
jerom ssi·neun oeguk chingu·ga isseoyo?
Jerome [polite][-topic] foreign-country friend-[subject] exist
Jerome, do you have foreign friends?

2 네, 저는 캐나다 친구하고 중국 친구가 있어요.
ne, jeo·neun kaenada chingu·hago jungguk chingu·ga isseoyo.
yes, I-[topic] Canada friend-and China friend-[subject] exist
Yes, I have Canadian and Chinese friends.

3 제 외국 친구들이 한국에 있어요.
je oeguk chingu·deur·i hangug·e isseoyo.
my foreign-country friend-[plural][subject] Korea[-place] exist
My foreign friends live in Korea.

1 *jay-rom shee-nuhn way-goo*[k] *chin-goo-ga eess-aw-yo* ***2*** *nay chaw-nuhn keh-na-da chin-goo-ha-go choong-goo*[k] *chin-goo-ga eess-aw-yo* ***3*** *chay way-goo*[k] *chin-goo-duhr-ee han-gook-ay eess-aw-yo*

Notes

In Korean, calling someone by the second-person pronoun *you* is avoided. Instead, the person's first name is used, followed by the polite term 씨 **-ssi** *[shee]*. This shows respect for the person being spoken to.

The particles 은 **-eun** *[uhn]* / 는 **-neun** *[nuhn]* indicate the topic of the sentence. (Note that the topic of a sentence is not necessarily the subject of the verb: the subject is indicated by the particles 이 **-i** *[ee]* / 가 **-ga** *[ga]*). Often, **-(n)eun** is used after a subject pronoun (*I, you, he, she*, etc.) if this refers to the topic of the sentence. The suffix 은 **-eun** is used if the pronoun (or noun) ends with a consonant, and 는 **-neun** is used if it ends with a vowel.

The first-person pronoun 저 **jeo** *[chaw]* can mean both *I* and *me*; the particle indicates whether it is a subject or object pronoun. The corresponding possessive adjective is 제 **je** *[chay]* *my*.

The coordinating conjunction 하고 **-hago** *[ha-go]* *and* is only used to link words. Another conjunction is used to link clauses.

If you want to emphasize that there are more than one of something, you can use the plural marker 들 **-deul** as a suffix attached to the noun. Its use is optional.

Practice – Translate the following sentences:

1. I have Canadian and American friends.
2. Jerome has Chinese friends.
3. 제 친구들이 한국에 있어요.
4. 저기에 제 미국 친구들이 있어요.

Answers:

1. 저는 캐나다 친구하고 미국 친구가 있어요.
2. 제롬 씨는 중국 친구가 있어요.
3. My friends live in Korea.
4. My American friends are over there.

Day 6

오늘 날씨가 어때요?
oneul nalssiga eottaeyo?
How is the weather today?

1 오늘 날씨가 좋아요.
oneul nalssi·ga joayo.
today weather-[subject] be-nice
It's nice today!

2 거리에 사람이 많아요.
geori·e saram·i manayo.
street-[place] person-[subject] be-many
There are lots of people in the street.

3 제주도가 정말 아름다워요.
jejudo·ga jeongmal areumdawoyo.
Jeju-island-[subject] really be-beautiful
Jeju Island is really beautiful.

4 서울이 요즘 더워요? 추워요?
seour·i yojeum deowoyo? chuwoyo?
Seoul-[subject] these-days be-hot? be-cold?
Is it hot or cold in Seoul at the moment?

***1** o-nuhl nal-shee-ga cho-a-yo **2** kaw-ree-ay sa-ram-ee man-a-yo **3** chay-joo-do-ga chawng-mal a-ruhm-da-wo-yo **4** saw-ool-ee yo-juhm daw-wo-yo? choo-wo-yo*

Notes

The impersonal pronoun *it* does not exist in Korean. The noun has to be used, followed by the particle marking it as a subject. We see this with *weather* in line 1: *It's nice.* ('weather-[subject] be-nice').

In Korean, adjectives function like verbs. They are in fact stative verbs, which are verbs that describe a state of being. This means that they take conjugation endings just like action verbs. In this lesson, the stative verbs are in the present (polite informal) tense: 좋아요 **joayo** *be nice, fine, good*; 많아요 **manayo** *be many*; 아름다워요 **areumdawoyo** *be beautiful*; 더워요 **deowoyo** *be hot*; 추워요 **chuwoyo** *be cold*.

The adverb 정말 **jeongmal** *really* usually comes before the verb (in this case, a stative verb).

Two questions one after the other automatically imply choice, so it isn't necessary to use *or* in Korean (line 4).

Practice – Translate the following sentences:

1. There are many people in the street today.
2. Is Korea beautiful?
3. 지하철에 사람이 많아요?
4. 요즘 정말 더워요.

Answers:

1. 오늘 거리에 사람이 많아요.
2. 한국이 아름다워요?
3. Are there many people in the metro?
4. It's really hot at the moment!

Day 7

식당에서 sikdangeseo
At the restaurant

1 무슨 한국 음식을 좋아해요?
museun hanguk eumsig·eul joahaeyo?
which Korea food-[object] like
Which Korean dish do you like?

2 불고기를 좋아해요. 아주 맛있어요.
bulgogi·reul joahaeyo. aju masisseoyo.
bulgogi-[object] like. very be-delicious
I like bulgogi. It is very tasty.

3 한국 식당이 여기에서 멀어요?
hanguk sikdang·i yeogi·eseo meoreoyo?
Korean restaurant-[subject] here-[place] be-far
Is the Korean restaurant far from here?

4 아니요. 안 멀어요. 바로 저기예요.
aniyo. an meoreoyo. baro jeogi·yeyo.
no. [not] be-far. just over-there-be
No, it's not far. It's just over there.

1 *moo-suhn han-goo*^{k} *uhm-sheek-uhl jo-a-heh-yo* ***2*** *pool-go-gee-ruhl jo-a-heh-yo. a-joo mash-eess-aw-yo* ***3*** *han-goo*^{k} *shi*^{k}*-tahng-ee yaw-kee-ay-saw mawr-aw-yo* ***4*** *a-nee-yo. an mawr-aw-yo. ba-ro chaw-gee-yay-yo*

Notes

The question word 무슨 **museun?** *Which? What?* is used with a noun (무슨 음식? *What food?*), whereas 무엇 **mueot?** is used with a verb (무엇이에요? *What is it?*).

Let's have a look at verb conjugation. A Korean verb in the infinitive form consists of the stem and the infinitive ending 다 **-da**: e.g. 좋아하다 **joahada** *to like, to love, to enjoy.* It does not conjugate for person, but has different forms to indicate tense and the degree of politeness: polite formal, polite informal or casual. In this phrasebook, we use polite informal, which is appropriate for most contexts. Regular verbs conjugate in the present tense polite informal by replacing the infinitive ending (다) with 아요 **-ayo** if the last vowel of the stem is ㅏ **a** or ㅗ **o**, or with 어요 **-eoyo** in all other cases.

Infinitive	Present tense (polite informal)
많다 **manda** *to be many*	많 + 아요 = 많아요 **manayo**
맛있다 **masitda** *to be delicious*	맛있 + 어요 = 맛있어요 **masisseoyo**
좋아하다 **joahada** *to like, to love*	좋아해요 **joahaeyo***

* irregular verb

The negation marker 안 **an** is placed before the verb it negates.

Practice–Translate the following sentences:

1. I like bulgogi.
2. Don't you like Korean food?
3. 멀어요?
4. 맛있어요?

Answers:

1. 불고기를 좋아해요.
2. 한국 음식을 안 좋아해요?
3. Is it far from here?
4. Is it delicious?

Day 8

영화관에서 yeonghwagwaneseo
At the cinema

1 커피숍에 갈까요? 영화관에 갈까요?
keopisyob·e ga·lkkayo? yeonghwagwan·e ga·lkkayo?
coffeeshop-[place] go-[request]? cinema-[place] go-[request]?
Shall we go to a coffee shop or the cinema?

2 음, 영화관에 가요. 한국 영화를 보고 싶어요.
eum, yeonghwagwan·e gayo. hanguk yeonghwa·reul bo·go sipeoyo.
hm, cinema-[place] go. Korea film-[object] watch-[want]
Hmm ... let's go to the cinema. I'd like to see a Korean film.

3 좋아요! 공포 영화를 볼까요?
joayo! gongpo yeonghwa·reul bo·lkkayo?
ok! horror film-[object] watch-[request]?
OK! How about watching a horror film?

1 *kaw-pee-shop-ay gal-κa-yo? yawng-hwa-gwan-ay gal-κa-yo* ***2*** *um, yawng-hwa-gwan-ay ka-yo. han-goo*[k] *yawng-hwa-ruhl po-go ship-aw-yo* ***3*** *cho-a-yo! kong-po yawng-hwa-ruhl pol-κa-yo*

Notes

A verb in Korean not only indicates tense and the degree of politeness, it also has endings that indicate grammatical mood (if something is a command, a suggestion, a declaration or a request).

A request is formed by replacing the infinitive ending with

을까요 **-eulkkayo** if the verb stem ends with a consonant or ㄹ까요 **-lkkayo** if it ends with a vowel:
가다 **gada** *to go* → 갈까요? **galkkayo?** *Shall we go?*
먹다 **meokda** *to eat* → 먹을까요? **meogeulkkayo?** *Shall we eat?* (the *[k]* sound becomes *[g]*).

To accept a request, you can simply use the polite informal ending (아요 **-ayo** / 어요 **-eoyo** in the present tense), which expresses all four moods – propositive (suggestion), declarative (statement), interrogative (question) and imperative (command): e.g. 가다 **gada** *to go* → 가요 **gayo** (가 **ga** + 아요 **ayo** becomes 가요 **gayo**; the 아 **a** of the ending is dropped). Depending on the context: *Let's go! I (you, etc.) go. Are you going?* or *Go away!*

There is also a verb ending for expressing a wish: 고 싶어요 **-go sipeoyo** *would like to, want to*. It replaces the infinitive ending: 보다 **boda** *to see, to watch* → 보고 싶어요 **bogo sipeoyo** *I'd like to see*; 먹다 **meokda** *to eat* → 먹고 싶어요 **meokgo sipeoyo** *I'd like to eat*.

Practice – Translate the following sentences:

1. I'd like to go to the cinema.
2. I'd like to eat bibimbap.
3. 한국에 갈까요?
4. 무엇을 하고 싶어요?

Answers:

1. 영화관에 가고 싶어요.
2. 비빔밥을 먹고 싶어요.
3. Shall we go to Korea?
4. What would you like to do?

Day 9

박물관에서 bangmulgwaneseo
At the museum

1 박물관에서 조용히 하세요.
bangmulgwan·eseo joyonghi ha·seyo.
museum-[place] silently do-[imperative]
Do not make noise in the museum.

2 작품을 만지지 마세요.
jakpum·eul manji·ji maseyo.
work-[object] touch-[prohibition]
Do not touch the artworks.

3 사진을 찍지 마세요.
sajin·eul jjik·ji maseyo.
photograph-[object] take-[prohibition]
Do not take photographs.

4 쓰레기를 버리지 마세요.
sseuregi·reul beori·ji maseyo.
garbage-[object] throw-away-[prohibition]
Do not litter.

***1** pahng-mool-gwan-ay-saw cho-yong-ee ha-say-yo **2** cha^{k}-poom-uhl man-jee-jee ma-say-yo **3** sa-jin-uhl CHik-jee ma-say-yo **4** suh-ray-gee-ruhl baw-ree-chee ma-say-yo*

Notes

A command can be softened by using an honorific to show respect. The compound form 으세요 **-euseyo** / 세요 **-seyo** is an

honorific imperative ending that combines the honorific infix 으시 **eusi** / 시 **si** (to convey deference towards the person being addressed) and the polite informal ending 어요 **-eoyo**. This gives a courteous tone to the command, equivalent to *please* in English. The polite informal ending on its own would express a direct order (or a statement, question or suggestion, depending on the context), so the honorific imperative is preferable if you want to be polite. If the verb stem ends with a consonant, use 으세요 **-euseyo**; if it ends with a vowel use 세요 **-seyo**:
e.g. 조용히 하다 **joyonghi ha**da *to be quiet* ('silently to-do') → 조용히 하세요 **joyonghi ha**seyo *Please be quiet!*

A prohibition is formed by replacing the infinitive ending with 지 마세요 **-ji maseyo** *do not*:
만지다 **manji**da *to touch* → 만지지 마세요 **manji**ji **maseyo** *Don't touch.*
사진을 찍다 **sajineul jjik**da *to take a photograph* → 사진을 찍지 마세요 **sajineul jjik**ji **maseyo** *Don't take photographs.*

Practice – Translate the following sentences:

1. Don't watch horror films.
2. Don't take photographs here.
3. 지하철에서 조용히 하세요.
4. 가지 마세요.

Answers:

1. 공포 영화를 보지 마세요.
2. 여기에서 사진을 찍지 마세요.
3. Be quiet in the metro.
4. Don't go there.

Day 10

호텔에서 hoteleseo
At the hotel

1 호텔 방을 예약해요.
hotel bang·eul yeyak·aeyo.
hotel room-[object] reservation-do
I reserve a hotel room.

2 욕실에서 샤워해요. 그리고 방에서 인터넷해요.
yoksir·eseo syawo·haeyo. geurigo bang·eseo inteonet·aeyo.
bathroom-[place] shower-do. and room[-place] internet-do
I take a shower in the bathroom and use the internet in the room.

3 조금 쉴 거예요. 이따가 쇼핑할 거예요.
jogeum swi·l geoyeyo. ittaga syopingha·l geoyeyo.
a-bit relax-[future]. later shopping-do-[future]
I'm going to rest a bit. I'll go shopping later.

***1** ho-tel pahng-uhl yay-yak-eh-yo **2** yok-shil-ay-saw sha-wo-heh-yo. kuh-ree-go pahng-ay-saw in-taw-nayt-eh-yo **3** cho-guhm sheel kaw-yay-yo. ee-TA-ga sho-ping-hal kaw-yay-yo*

Notes

The verb 하다 **hada** *to do* is a very important word in Korean. It can be combined with many nouns to turn them into verbs: e.g. 인터넷하다 (인터넷 *internet* + 하다 *to do*) → 인터넷해요 **inteonetaeyo** *I* (*you*, etc.) *use the internet*. The verb **hada** is irregular, so in the polite informal present it is 해요 **haeyo** (an **e** is added before the **yo**).

Note that the initial ㅎ **h** is silent after certain consonants, so in the Romanization it is transliterated as **aeyo**.

The coordinating conjunction 그리고 **geurigo** *and* can be used to link clauses as well as words. (The conjunction 하고 **-hago** *and* is used only to link words—see Day 5.)

In line 3 we see the future tense. This is formed by replacing the infinitive ending of the verb with ㄹ **-l** / 을 **-eul** 거예요 **geoyeyo**. If the verb stem ends with a vowel use -ㄹ 거예요 **-l geoyeyo**; if it ends with a consonant use -을 거예요 **-eul geoyeyo**:
쉬다 **swida** *[shee-da] to rest, relax* → 쉴 거예요 **swil geoyeyo** *I (you, etc.) will rest*
먹다 **meokda** *to eat* → 먹을 거예요 **meogeul geoyeyo** *I (you, etc.) will eat*.

Practice—Translate the following sentences:

1. I'm going to go to the cinema today.
2. I'd like to reserve a hotel room.
3. 이따가 한국 식당에 갈 거예요.
4. 슈퍼에서 음료수를 살 거예요.

Answers:

1. 오늘 영화관에 갈 거예요.
2. 호텔 방을 예약하고 싶어요.
3. I will go to the Korean restaurant later.
4. I'll buy a drink at the supermarket.

Day 11

서울에서 seouleseo
In Seoul

1 어제 인사동에서 기념품을 샀어요.
eoje insadong·eseo ginyeompum·eul sa·sseoyo.
yesterday Insa-district-[place] souvenir-[object] buy-[past]
Yesterday I bought souvenirs in Insa-dong.

2 오늘 친구를 만나요. 친구하고 한강에 가요.
oneul chingu·reul mannayo. chingu·hago hangang·e gayo.
today friend-[object] meet. friend-with Han-river-[place] go
Today I'm meeting friends. I'm going to the Han River with them.

3 내일 아마도 동대문에 갈 거예요.
naeil amado dongdaemun·e ga·l geoyeyo.
tomorrow perhaps Dongdaemun-[place] go-[future]
Tomorrow maybe I will go to Dongdaemun.

***1** aw-jay in-sa-dong-ay-saw gee-nyawm-poom-uhl sass-aw-yo **2** o-nuhl chin-goo-ruhl man-na-yo. chin-goo-ha-go han-gahng-ay ka-yo **3** neh-il a-ma-do tong-deh-moon-ay kal kaw-yay-yo*

Notes

As you know, the present polite informal ends in 어요 **-eoyo** / 아요 **-ayo** (line 2). This can translate to the English simple present (*I go*) or the present continuous (*I'm going*).

The past (e.g. *I went*) is indicated by the suffix 았 **-at** or 었 **-eot** (the **t** sound becomes **ss**), followed by the polite informal suffix 어요 **-eoyo**. So if the last vowel of the stem is ㅏ **a** or ㅗ **o**, the past polite informal suffix is 았어요 **-asseoyo**; in all other cases it is 었어요 **-eosseoyo**:

사다 **sada** *to buy* → 샀어요 **sasseoyo** (the 아 **a** of the ending is dropped) *I* (*you*, etc.) *bought*

먹다 **meokda** *to eat* → 먹었어요 **meogeosseoyo** *I* (*you*, etc.) *ate*.

Some good news: there is only one past tense form–there is no distinction between *I ate* and *I have eaten*.

When the conjunction 하고 **-hago** is attached as a suffix to a noun referring to a person, it means *with*: e.g. 친구하고 **chinguhago** *with a/some/my friend(s)*; 캐롤하고 **kaerolhago** *with Carol*.

Practice–Translate the following sentences:

1. Tomorrow I'll reserve a hotel room.
2. Yesterday I took photos in Seoul.
3. 어제 날씨가 좋았어요.
4. 어제 식당에서 한국 음식을 먹었어요. 아주 맛있었어요.

Answers:

1. 내일 호텔 방을 예약할 거예요.
2. 어제 서울에서 사진을 찍었어요.
3. Yesterday the weather was nice.
4. Yesterday I ate Korean food at a restaurant. It was very tasty.

↗ Day 12

숫자 **sutja** ('number')
Counting: the Korean system

1 몇 시예요?
myeot si·yeyo?
what time-be
What time is it?

2 오후 두 시예요.
ohu du si·yeyo.
afternoon two o'clock-be
It's 2 p.m.

3 몇 살이에요?
myeot sar·ieyo?
what age-be
How old are you?

4 스물 다섯 살이에요.
seumul daseot sar·ieyo.
twenty five age-be
I'm 25 years old.

5 가방에 선글라스 세 개가 있어요.
gabang·e seongeullaseu se gae·ga isseoyo.
bag-[place] sunglasses three [classifier]-[subject] exist
There are three pairs of sunglasses in my bag.

***1** myaw[t] shee-yay-yo **2** o-hoo too shee-yay-yo **3** myaw[t] sar-ee-ay-yo **4** suh-muhl ta-saw[t] sar-ee-ay-yo **5** ka-bahng-ay sun-guhl-la-s say keh-ga eess-aw-yo*

Notes

There are two counting systems in Korean: one is purely Korean and one is Sino-Korean (more on this in the next lesson). Each system is used in specific contexts. The Korean system is used only for three things: the hour (the Sino-Korean system is used for minutes), age and countable objects.

The day is divided into 오전 **ojeon** *the morning* and 오후 **ohu** *the*

afternoon; these terms are used to specify the 12-hour period of the day and come before the time:
오후 다섯 시 **ohu daseot si** *5:00 p.m.* ('afternoon 5 o'clock')
오전 다섯 시 **ojeon daseot si** *5:00 a.m.* ('morning 5 o'clock').

When the quantity of an object or a countable living thing is given, a classifier (also known as a measure word) is used after the number. There are different classifiers depending on the type of thing being counted: e.g. 명 **myeong** is used for people; 마리 **mari** is used for animals; 대 **dae** for electrical equipment and vehicles; and 개 **gae** for most other objects. The word order is item + Korean number + classifier:
e.g. 선글라스 세 개 **seongeullaseu se gae** *three pairs of sunglasses* ('sunglass three [item]').

Note that the numbers *1* **hana**, *2* **dul**, *3* **set** and *4* **net** drop the final letter when followed by a noun: *1* 개 **han gae**, *2* 개 **du gae**, *3* 개 **se gae**, *4* 개 **ne gae**.

Practice – Translate the following sentences:

1. It is 2 p.m.
2. I have three Korean friends.
3. 스물 다섯 살이에요.
4. 택시 다섯 대가 있어요.

Answers:

1. 오후 두 시예요.
2. 한국 친구 세 명이 있어요.
3. I'm 25 years old.
4. There are five taxis.

↗ Day 13

숫자 **sutja** ('number')
Counting: the Sino-Korean system

1 오후 네 시 삼십 분에 기차역에서 만나요.
ohu ne si samsip bun·e gichayeog·eseo mannayo.
afternoon 4 o'clock 30 minutes-[time] station-[place] meet
Let's meet at 4:30 p.m. at the station.

2 제 생일은 6월 16일이에요.
je saengir·eun yu·wol sibyuk·ir·ieyo.
my birthday-[topic] 6-month 16-day-be
My birthday is the 16th of June.

3 사십 팔 번 버스를 타세요.
sasip pal beon beoseu·reul ta·seyo.
40 8 number bus-[object] ride-[imperative]
Take bus number 48.

1 *o-hoo nay shee sam-ship poon-ay kee-cha-yawk-ay-saw man-na-yo* ***2*** *chay seng-eel-uhn yoo-wol shim-yook il ee-ay-yo* ***3*** *sa- ship pal pawn baw-suh-ruhl ta-say-yo*

Notes

While the purely Korean numbers are used for the hour, age and countable objects, the Sino-Korean numbers are used for everything else, i.e. minutes, telephone numbers, dates, prices, bus or metro numbers, etc. From 100, only the Sino-Korean counting system is used.

So giving the time requires both systems: the Korean number for the hour and the Sino-Korean number for the minutes. As in

English, you can use the term for *half* (반 **ban**) with times: 오후 네 시 반 **ohu ne si ban** *4:30 p.m.* or *half past four in the afternoon* ('afternoon 4 o'clock half').

To give the date you simply use the Sino-Korean number suffixed with the corresponding temporal term, following the order year-month-day: 년 **-nyeon** *year*, 월 **-wol** *month*, 일 **-il** *day*: e.g. 2016 년 12 월 25 일 *December 25, 2016*.

Here are the months:

Jan	1월 **irwol** *[eel-wol]*	*July*	7월 **chirwol** *[chi'-"]*
Feb	2월 **iwol** *[ee-"]*	*Aug*	8월 **parwol** *[pa'-"]*
March	3월 **samwol** *[sam-"]*	*Sept*	9월 **guwol** *[koo-"]*
April	4월 **sawol** *[sa-"]*	*Oct*	10월 **siwol** *[shee-"]*
May	5월 **owol** *[oh-"]*	*Nov*	11월 **sibirwol** *[shibir-"]*
June	6월 **yuwol** *[yoo-"]*	*Dec*	12월 **sibiwol** *[shibee-"]*

The same particle 에 **-e** is used to indicate destination and time. Don't forget the useful possessive adjective 제 **je** *my*.

Practice – Translate the following sentences:

1. How about meeting at the cinema at 4:30 p.m.?
2. My birthday is October 30.
3. 몇 시에 기차를 타요?
4. 한 시 반에 기차를 타요.

Answers:

1. 오후 네 시 반에 영화관에서 만날까요?
2. 제 생일은 시월 삼십일이에요.
3. What time do you take the train?
4. I take my train at 1:30 p.m.

Day 14

가게에서 gageeseo
At the store

1 어서 오세요. 무엇을 찾으세요?
eoseo o·seyo. mueos·eul chaj·euseyo?
quick come-[imperative]. what-[object] search-[interrogative]
Welcome, sir/ma'am. What are you looking for?

2 치약 한 개 하고 칫솔 두 개 주세요.
chiyak han gae hago chitsol du gae ju·seyo.
toothpaste one [classif.] and toothbrush two [classif.] give-[imperative]
A tube of toothpaste and two toothbrushes, please.

3 여기요. 감사합니다. 안녕히 가세요.
yeogi·yo. gamsahamnida. annyeonghi ga·seyo.
here-[polite]. thank you. goodbye leave-[imperative]
Here you are. Thank you. Goodbye.

***1** aw-saw o-say-yo. moo-aws-uhl chaj-uh-say-yo **2** chee-ya[k] han keh ha-go chi[t]-sol doo keh choo-say-yo **3** yaw-kee-yo. kam-sa-am-nee-da. an-nyawng-ee ka-say-yo*

Notes

The honorific infix 으시 **eusi** / 시 **si** expresses respect towards the person being spoken to. In Korean culture it is used to address parents, teachers, managers, customers, clients, etc. It should not be used to speak about oneself. Any verb or adjective can be made into an honorific form by adding this infix after the stem and before the ending. If the stem ends with a consonant, use 으시 **eusi**; if it ends with a vowel, use 시 **si**.

In this lesson, the honorific infix is followed by the polite verb ending 어요 **-eoyo**. When the infix and verb ending are combined, the suffix becomes 으세요 **-euseyo** (after a consonant) or 세요 **-seyo** (after a vowel): e.g. 무엇을 찾다 **mueoseul chatda** *to look for something* → 무엇을 찾으세요 **mueoseul chajeuseyo?** *What are you looking for?*; 주다 **juda** *to give* → 주세요 **juseyo** *Please give me ....* (both forms are courteous). See also Day 9.

The polite suffix 요 **-yo** is attached to the end of a noun to show courtesy and respect. For example, the answer to the question *Who wants some cheese?* would be 저요 **jeoyo!** *Me!* (politely).

Practice–Translate the following sentences:

1. Welcome.
2. Which place are you looking for?
3. 누구를 찾으세요?
4. 선글라스 한 개 주세요.

Answers:

1. 어서 오세요.
2. 어디를 찾으세요?
3. Who are you looking for?
4. Give me a pair of sunglasses, please.

Day 15

우체국에서 uchegugeseo
At the post office

1 가족에게 엽서를 보내야 해요. 어디에 가야 해요?
gajog·ege yeopseo·reul bonae·ya haeyo. eodi·e ga·ya haeyo?
family-[indirect object] postcard-[direct object] send-must. where-[destination] go-must
I have to send a postcard to my family. Where should I go?

2 우체국에 가세요. 거기에서 보낼 수 있어요.
uchegug·e ga·seyo. geogi·eseo bonae·l su isseoyo.
post-office-[destination] go-[imperative]. there-[place] send can
Go to the post office. You can send it from there.

3 어디에서 돈을 찾을 수 있어요?
eodi·eseo don·eul chaj·eul su isseoyo?
where-[place] money-[object] find can
Where can I withdraw money?

1 *ka-jok-ay-kay yawp-saw-ruhl bo-neh-ya heh-yo. aw-dee-ay ka-ya heh-yo* ***2*** *oo-chay-gook-ay ka-say-yo. kaw-kee-ay-saw po-ne' soo eess-aw-yo* ***3*** *aw-dee-ay-saw tohn-uhl chaj-uhl soo eess-aw-yo*

Notes

To express obligation (*must*, *have to*), the ending 아야 **-aya** / 어야 **-eoya** 해요 **haeyo** replaces the infinitive ending of the verb. If the last vowel of the stem is ㅏ **a** or ㅗ **o**, use 아야 **-aya**; after any other vowel, use 어야 **-eoya**. If the stem ends with the same vowel as the one the ending starts with, the first vowel sound of

the ending (아 **a** or 어 **eo)** is dropped:
보내다 **bonaeda** *to send* → 보내야 해요 **bonaeya haeyo** (어 **eo** is omitted) *must send*
가다 **gada** *to go* → 가야 해요 **gaya haeyo** (아 **a** is omitted) *must go*.

The particle 에게 **-ege** indicates an indirect object (a noun that indirectly receives the action of the verb–often a person, i.e. *to him, to her, to them*, etc.). The same form is used regardless of the last letter of the noun.

To express possibility (*can, could)*, the ending ㄹ **-l** / 을 **-eul** 수 있어요 **su isseoyo** replaces the infinitive ending. If the stem ends with a vowel, use ㄹ 수 있어요 **-l su isseoyo**; if it ends with a consonant, use 을 수 있어요 **-eul su isseoyo**:
보내다 **bonaeda** *to send* → 보낼 수 있어요 **bonael su isseoyo** *can send*
찾다 **chatda** *to find* → 찾을 수 있어요 **chajeul su isseoyo** *can find, can look for*.

Practice–Translate the following sentences:

1. Can I take a photo here?
2. Where can I buy a postcard?
3. 우체국에서 돈을 찾을 수 있어요?
4. 우체국에서 엽서를 보낼 수 있어요.

Answers:

1. 여기에서 사진을 찍을 수 있어요?
2. 어디에서 엽서를 살 수 있어요?
3. Can I withdraw money at the post office?
4. You can send a postcard at the post office.

Day 16

한국 음식 hanguk eumsik
Korean food

1 맛이 어때요?
mas·i eottaeyo?
taste-[subject] be-how
How does it taste?

2 잠깐만요. 지금 맛보고 있어요.
jamkkanman·yo. jigeum matbo·go isseoyo.
one-moment-[polite]. now tasting-be in-act-of
One moment, please. I'm just trying it now.

3 음... 맵지만 맛있어요.
eum... maep·jiman masisseoyo.
hmm... be-spicy-but be-delicious
Hmm ... it's spicy but delicious!

***1** mas-ee aw-Teh-yo **2** cham-Kan-man-yo. chee-kuhm ma[t]-po-ko eess-aw-yo **3** um... meh[p]-chee-man mash-eess-aw-yo*

Notes

To ask an opinion, the stative verb 어떻다 **eotteota** *be how* is used. (A stative verb is a verb that describes a state rather than an action.) This is an irregular verb, so in the present polite informal it is 어때요 **eottaeyo**.

The present continuous (or present progressive) is a tense used to indicate being in the middle of something or currently in the process of something (*to be ... -ing*). In Korean, the ending

고 있어요 **-go isseoyo** *to be in the process of* replaces the infinitive ending of the verb, regardless of the last letter of the stem: e.g. 맛보다 **matboda** *to taste* → 맛보고 있어요 **matbogo isseoyo** *I am tasting, you are tasting, he/she is tasting,* etc.

The connecting word 지만 **-jiman** *but, though* is attached to the previous word: e.g. 맵다 **maepda** *to be spicy* → 맵지만 **maepjiman** *it is spicy, but ...*

Practice–Translate the following sentences:

1. How do you like Seoul?
2. I'm watching a film.
3. 한국 음식이 어때요?
4. 한국 음식이 맵지만 맛있어요.

Answers:

1. 서울이 어때요?
2. 영화를 보고 있어요.
3. How do you like Korean food?
4. Korean food is spicy, but it's delicious.

Day 17

옷 가게에서 ot gageeseo
At the clothing store

1 이 옷 좀 입어 볼 수 있어요?
i ot jom ibeo bo·l su isseoyo?
this clothing try put-on see-can
Can I try this item of clothing on?

2 당연하죠. 한 번 입어 보세요.
dangyeonha·jyo. han beon ibeo bo·seyo.
be-obvious-[polite]. one time try see-[imperative]
Of course! Try it on.

3 예쁜데 가격이 비싸네요. 좀 깎아 주세요.
yeppeu·nde gagyeog·i bissa·neyo. jom kkakk·a juseyo.
be-pretty-but price-[subject] be-expensive-[surprise]. a-bit reduce-[honorific imperative]
It's pretty, but expensive. Could you give me a discount?

1 *ee o*[t] *chom eeb-aw pol soo eess-aw-yo* ***2*** *tahng-yawn-ha-jyo. han pawn eeb-aw po-say-yo* ***3*** *yay-ᴘuhn-day ka-gyaw*[k]*-ee pee-ssa-nay-yo. chom ᴋaᴋ-a joo-say-yo*

Notes

The little word 이 **i** means *this, these*. It comes before the noun: 이 옷 **i ot** *these clothes*; 이 친구 **i chingu** *this friend*.

The final ending 죠 **-jyo** is a shortened form of 지요 **-jiyo**. It is added to the stem of a word to informally express politeness and respect. It is often used in spoken language. We see another final ending in line 3, 네요 **-neyo**, which is also used in spoken language. It's tricky to translate, but conveys a nuance of surprise.

The connecting word ㄴ데 **-nde** / 은데 **-eunde** *but, however, though* is attached to the stem of a stative verb to introduce a contrasting idea. Use ㄴ데 **-nde** if the stem ends with a vowel, and 은데 **-eunde** if it ends with a consonant. It's identical to 지만 **jiman** *but*, but is used mainly in spoken language.

The expression 좀 **jom** + (verb stem + 아 **-a** / 어 **-eo**) 주세요 **juseyo** is often used in everyday speech to soften a request. If the last vowel of the verb stem is ㅏ **a** or ㅗ **o**, use 아 주세요 **-a juseyo**; after any other vowel use 어 주세요 **-eo juseyo**:
e.g. 깎다 **kkakda** *to reduce a price* → 좀 깎아 주세요 **jom kkakka juseyo** *Could you reduce the price, please?*

Practice–Translate the following sentences:

1. Could you give me a discount, please?
2. These clothes are really pretty.
3. 한 번 입어 보세요.
4. 비싸네요.

Answers:

1. 좀 깎아 주세요.
2. 이 옷이 정말 예쁘네요.
3. Try it on.
4. It's expensive.

Day 18

약국에서 yakgukeseo
At the pharmacy

1 어떻게 오셨어요?
eotteoke o·sy·eosseoyo?
how come-[honorific][past]
Can I help you?

2 머리가 아파서 왔는데요.
meori·ga ap·aseo wan·neundeyo.
head-[subject] be-sick-[cause] come-[past]-[...]
I've come because I have a headache ...

3 머리가 아프면 두통약을 드세요.
meori·ga apeu·myeon dutongyag·eul deu·seyo.
head-[subject] be-sick-if headache-pill-[object] take-[imperative]
If you have a headache, take a pain relief tablet.

1 *aw-taw-kay o-sheeawss-aw-yo* ***2*** *maw-ree-ga a-pa-saw wat-nuhn-day-yo* ***3*** *maw-ree-ga a-puh-myawn doo-tong-yak-uhl duh-say-yo*

Notes

Remember that the past polite informal suffix is 았어요 **-asseoyo** (after ㅏ **a** or ㅗ **o**) or 었어요 **-eosseoyo** (see Day 11), and the honorific infix is 으시 **eusi** (after a consonant) or 시 **si** (see Day 14). So in line 1 we have:
오다 **oda** *to come* → 오셨어요 **osyeosseoyo** (오 **o** + honorific infix 시 **si** + past polite informal suffix 었어요 **-eosseoyo**) *you (he, she,* etc.) *came*.

The connecting word 아서 **-aseo** (after ㅏ **a** or ㅗ **o**) / 어서 **-eoseo** (after other vowels) *because* is added to the stem of a verb/adjective. But note that verb stems ending in **eu** drop the latter before adding the suffix: e.g. 아프다 **apeuda** *to be sick* → 아파서 **apaseo** *because I am (you are,* etc.) *sick*.

In spoken language, the final ending 는데요 **-neundeyo** can be added to the stem of an action verb to convey that the action is continuing into the present. It expresses willingness to continue the conversation and softens the phrase.

The connecting word 으면 **-eumyeon** (after a consonant) / 면 **-myeon** (after a vowel) *if* is added to the stem of the verb/adjective: e.g. 아프다 **apeuda** *to be sick* → 아프면 **apeumyeon** *if I am (you are,* etc.) *sick*.

Practice–Translate the following sentences:

1. I bought these clothes because they're pretty.
2. Rest if you're sick.
3. 날씨가 좋으면 친구를 만날 거예요.
4. 맛있어서 비빔밥을 좋아해요.

Answers:

1. 예뻐서 이 옷을 샀어요.
2. 아프면 쉬세요.
3. If it's nice, I'll go see my friends.
4. I like bibimbap because it's delicious.

Day 19

놀이 nori
Recreation

1 노래부르러 노래방에 가요.
noraebureu·reo norae·bang·e gayo.
sing-for song-room-[destination] go
To sing, I go to a karaoke box.

2 쉬러 찜질방에 가요.
swi·reo jjimjil·bang·e gayo.
rest-for heating-room-[destination] go
To relax, I go to the public bathhouse.

3 게임하러 게임방에 가요.
geimha·reo geim·bang·e gayo.
play-game-for game-room-[destination] go
To play games, I go to the game room.

4 와! 재미있을 것 같아요.
wa! jaemiiss·eul geot gatayo.
wow! be-entertaining-I think
Wow! That sounds fun!

1 *no-reh-boo-ruh-raw no-reh-bahng-ay ka-yo* ***2*** *shwee-raw cHim-jil-bahng-ay ka-yo* ***3*** *kay-eem-a-raw kay-eem-pahng-ay ka-yo* ***4*** *wa! cheh-mee-eess-uhl kaw[t] kat-a-yo*

Notes

The connecting word 으러 **-eureo** (after a consonant) / 러 **-reo** (after a vowel) *for (the purpose of), (in order) to* is often used with verbs of movement such as 가다 **gada** *to go* / 오다 **oda** *to come* to indicate the purpose of the action: 먹다 **meokda** *to eat* → 먹으러 **meogeureo** *in order to eat*; 노래부르다 **noraebureuda** *to sing* → 노래부르러 **noraebureureo** *in order to sing*.

The word 방 **bang** literally means *room*. In South Korea, many leisure or recreational places include this term. For example, a 찜질방 **jjimjilbang** is a Korean bathhouse with hot tubs, traditional dry kiln saunas, ice rooms, exercise rooms, massage tables, and rooms for lounging and sleeping, watching TV and eating. A uniform is provided at the entrance, usually blue for men and pink for women (only the bath areas are gender segregated).

To give an opinion (*I think*, *it seems*, *that looks*, etc.), ㄹ **-l** (after a vowel) / 을 **-eul** (after a consonant) 것 같아요 **geot gatayo** is added to the stem of a verb/adjective: e.g. 재미있다 **jaemiitda** *to be fun* → 재미있을 것 같아요 **jaemiisseul geot gatayo** *that sounds/looks/seems fun*.

Practice–Translate the following sentences:

1. The bulgogi looks delicious.
2. I'm going to the supermarket to buy some drinks.
3. 무엇하러 찜질방에 가요?
4. 게임하러 갈까요?

Answers:

1. 불고기가 맛있을 것 같아요.
2. 음료수를 사러 슈퍼에 가요.
3. For what purpose are you going to the bathhouse?
4. Shall we go play some games?

Day 20

큰 가방 keun gabang
A large bag

1 큰 가방 / 작은 지갑 / 예쁜 신발
keu·n gabang / jag·eun jigap / yeppeu·n sinbal
large-[adj.] bag / small-[adj.] wallet / pretty-[adj.] shoes
large bag / small wallet / pretty shoes

2 컴퓨터하는 남자 / 빵을 먹는 여자
keompyuteo·ha·neun namja / ppang·eul meong·neun yeoja
computer-do-[clause] man / bread-[object] eat-[clause] woman
a man who uses the computer / a woman who eats bread

***1** kuhn ka-bahng / chahg-uhn chee-ga[p] / yay-Puhn shin-bal **2** kawm-pyoo-taw-ha-nuhn nam-ja / Pahng-uhl mawng-nuhn yaw-ja*

Notes

As we've seen, adjectives in Korean often function as verbs, e.g. 크다 **keuda** *to be large*. To use an adjective to describe a noun (i.e. without the meaning 'is'), the suffix ㄴ **-n** (after a vowel) or 은 **-eun** (after a consonant) is added to the stem:
e.g. 예쁘다 **yeppeuda** *to be pretty* → 예쁜 **yeppeun** 신발 **sinbal** *pretty shoes*.

In Korean, a verb + object can be turned into a clause that describes a noun using the suffix 는 **-neun**. In English, this is usually achieved with a relative clause (the extra information about a noun follows *that, who, which*, etc.). In Korean, the construction is noun + stem of present tense action verb + suffix

는 **-neun**: e.g. 빵을 먹다 **ppangeul meokda** *to eat bread* + 여자 **yeoja** *woman* → 빵을 먹는 여자 **ppangeul meongneun yeoja** *a woman who eats bread.*

To use a phrase like this in a sentence, imagine the different elements as building blocks:
빵을 먹는 여자 **ppangeul meongneun yeoja** ('bread-[object] eat-[clause] woman') + 을 **-eul** / 를 **-reul** 만나요 **mannayo** ('-[object] meet') → 빵을 먹는 여자를 만나요 **ppangeul meongneun yeojareul mannayo.** *I am meeting the woman who eats bread.*

Practice–Translate the following sentences:

1. a large bag
2. I like large bags.
3. 비빔밥을 좋아하는 친구
4. 비빔밥을 좋아하는 친구를 만나요.

Answers:

1. 큰 가방
2. 큰 가방을 좋아해요.
3. a friend who likes bibimbap
4. I'm going to see a friend who likes bibimbap.

Day 21

출발 **chulbal**
The departure

1 빨리요! 늦을지 몰라요.
ppalli·yo! neuj·eulji mollayo.
quick-[polite]! be-late-[uncertainty]
Hurry! We might be late.

2 좀 더 자고 싶은데...기차가 몇 시에 출발하나요?
jom deo ja·go sip·eunde...gicha·ga myeot si·e chulbalha·nayo?
a-bit more sleep-[want]-[...!]... train-[subject] what time-[time] leave-[?]
I want to sleep a bit more ... What time does the train leave?

3 곧 출발한다니까요.
got chulbalha·ndanikkayo.
soon leave-[I said]
As I told you, it leaves soon.

***1** ppal-lee-yo! nuhj-uhl-chee mol-la-yo **2** chom taw cha-go ship-uhn-day...kee-cha-ga myaw[t] shi-ay chool-bal-ha-na-yo **3** ko[t] chool-bal-han-da-nee-kka-yo*

Notes

To convey doubt or uncertainty (*I think that, I don't know if, I'm not sure if*, etc.), ㄹ지 **-lji** (after a vowel) / 을지 **-eulji** (after a consonant) 몰라요 **mollayo** is added to the verb stem:
늦다 **neutda** *to be late* → 늦을지 몰라요 **neujeulji mollayo** *I think we're going to be late. We might be late.*
자다 **jada** *to sleep* → 잘지 몰라요 **jalji mollayo** *I don't know if he/she is sleeping. He/she might be sleeping.*

With a verb describing a state, the final ending ㄴ **-n** (after a vowel) / 은데 **-eunde** (after a consonant) can be added to the stem to both elicit a response from the listener and to express surprise, interest, an exclamation, etc.: e.g. 자고 싶다 **jago sipda** *I'd like to sleep* → 자고 싶은데 **jago sipeunde** *I'd like to sleep ...!* (Remember the verb ending 고 싶어요 **-go sipeoyo** *would like to, want to* from Day 8?)

The final ending 나요 **-nayo** is added to a verb stem to indicate a query. It is often used in spoken language to ask a question about something one isn't sure of or is curious about.

The final ending ㄴ **-n** (after a vowel) / 는 **-neun** (after a consonant) 다니까요 **danikkayo** is added to the verb stem to repeat something, emphasizing that it has been previously said (i.e. *I told you, I said*).

Practice – Translate the following sentences:

1. I don't know if it will be nice tomorrow.
2. I'd like to go to Korea ...!
3. 기차가 곧 출발하나요?
4. 늦는다니까요.

Answers:

1. 내일 날씨가 좋을지 모르겠어요.
2. 한국에 가고 싶은데...
3. Is the train leaving soon?
4. As I told you, we are (*I am, you are,* etc.) late.

Conversing

First contact

Greetings

In Korean, 안녕하세요? **annyeonghaseyo?** *Hello!* is a question. It derives from the verb 안녕하다 **annyeonghada** *be at peace* ('peace-be') and literally enquires if someone is untroubled. The shorter greeting 안녕? **annyeong?** *Hi!* is only used in casual contexts with peers or very close friends or family.

Hello! / Good morning!	안녕하세요? **annyeonghaseyo?**	*an-nyawng-a-say-yo*
Hi! (very informal)	안녕? **annyeong?**	*an-nyawng*

How are you?

잘 지내세요?
jal jinaeseyo?
chal chee-neh-say-yo
well pass

요즘 어떻게 지내세요?
yojeum eotteoke jinaeseyo?
yo-juhm aw-TAW-kay chee-neh-say-yo
these-days how pass

Saying goodbye

Depending on whether a person is the one staying or leaving, there are two ways to say goodbye: 안녕히 계세요 **annyeonghi gyeseyo** 'stay well' (said when leaving) and 안녕히 가세요 **annyeonghi gaseyo** 'go well' (said when staying behind).

See you again soon!	또 봐요. **tto bwayo**	*TOH pa-yo*
See you tomorrow!	내일 봐요. **naeil bwayo**	*neh-eel pa-yo*
See you next time!	다음에 봐요. **daeume bwayo**	*ta-uhm-ay pa-yo*
See you later!	이따 봐요. **itta bwayo**	*ee-TA pa-yo*

Goodbye! (when leaving)	안녕히 계세요. **annyeonghi gyeseyo**	*an-nywang-ee kay-say-yo*
Goodbye! (when staying)	안녕히 가세요. **annyeonghi gaseyo**	*an-nyawng-ee ka-say-yo*

Thanking, apologizing and excusing

Rather than saying 'You're welcome. It's nothing.' Koreans usually just give a small smile.

Thank you.	고마워요. **gomawoyo**	*ko-ma-wo-yo*
You're welcome. (formal) / (informal)	천만에요. **cheonmaneyo /** 뭘요. **mworyo**	*chawn-man-ay-yo / mol-yo*
I'm sorry. (formal) / (informal)	죄송합니다. **joesonghamnida /** 미안해요. **mianhaeyo**	*chay-song-am-nee-da / mee-an-heh-yo*
Excuse me ... (formal)	실례지만... **sillyejiman**	*shil-lay-jee-man*
Excuse me! (to catch attention)	여기요! / 저기요! **yeogiyo / jeogiyo**	*yaw-gee-yo / chaw-gee-yo*

Offering wishes

You might hear 수고 하세요 **sugo haseyo** ('effort make'), which is said when leaving the workplace to those who remain. It means something like *Keep up the good work!* but is used almost like *Have a good day!* when taking leave of someone. It is very common because Koreans spend a lot of time at work!

Keep up the good work! / Take care!	수고 하세요. **sugo haseyo**	*soo-go ha-say-yo*
Cheer up!	힘 내세요. **him naeseyo**	*heem neh-say-yo*
Congratulations! (informal) / (formal)	축하해요. **chukahaeyo/** 축하드려요. **chukadeuryeoyo**	*chook-a-eh-yo / chook-a-duh-raw-yo*

Happy Birthday!	생일 축하해요. **saengil chukahaeyo**	seng-il chook-a-eh-yo
Happy New Year!	새해 복 많이 받으세요. **saehae bok mani badeuseyo**	*seh-heh po^{k} man-ee pad-uh-say-yo*

Agreeing and disagreeing

Avoid simply using 'yes' or 'no' on its own, as this suggests a lack of desire to continue the conversation, or even rejection in the case of 'no'.

Yes.	네. **ne**	*nay*
Yes, of course!	네, 당연하죠. **ne, dangyeonhajyo**	*nay tahng-yawn-a-jo*
Yes, I understand.	네, 알겠어요. **ne, algesseoyo**	*nay al-gayss-aw-yo*
All right.	좋아요. **joayo**	*cho-ah-yo*
Well ... I'll think about it.	글쎄요, 생각해 볼게요. **geulsseyo, saenggakae bolgeyo**	*kuhl-say-yo seng-gak-eh pol-kay-yo*
I'm not sure.	잘 모르겠어요. **jal moreugesseoyo**	*chal mo^{l}-ruh-gayss-aw-yo*
I don't think so.	아닌 것 같은데요. **anin geot gateundeyo**	*a-neen gaw^{t} kat-uhn-day-yo*
No.	아니요. **aniyo**	*a-nee-yo*
No, thank you.	아니요, 괜찮아요. **aniyo, gwaenchanayo**	*a-nee-yo kwen-chan-a-yo*

Asking questions

As with agreeing or disagreeing, it is abrupt in Korean culture to respond with a one-word answer if someone asks you a question. You should repeat the verb used in the question when answering, e.g. *Yes, I am.* rather than simply *Yes.*

Are you a student?
학생이에요?
haksaengieyo?
hak-seng-ee-ay-yo
student-be

Yes, I'm a student.
네, 학생이에요.
ne, haksaengieyo.
nay hak-seng-ee-ay-yo
yes, student-be

No, I'm not a student.
아니요, 학생이 아니에요.
aniyo, haksaengi anieyo.
a-nee-yo hak-seng-ee a-nee-ay-yo
no, student not-be

Here are some questions you can use in conversations (see also the back cover flap for common question words):

Ah! Is that so?	아! 그래요? **a! geuraeyo?**	*ah kuh-reh-yo*
Really?	정말요? **jeongmaryo?**	*chawng-mal-yo*

Body language

Westerners frequently use gestures and facial expressions to animate a conversation. Koreans (like other Confucian cultures) tend not to. A Confucian ideal is 'discreetness': being showy or calling attention to yourself is to be avoided. This is why Korean women cover their mouth when they laugh.

In Korea, never point at someone with your finger. It is also advisable to avoid looking directly into someone's eyes when speaking to them. This can be interpreted as rude or even as a provocation. Look at the chin instead, occasionally glancing at the eyes. Koreans greet each other with a slight bow; they don't hug, kiss or pat backs or shoulders. If you shake someone's hand, it is best to use both hands–this is a sign of respect.

Making yourself understood

I speak Korean.
한국어를 할 수 있어요.
hangugeoreul hal su isseoyo.
han-goog-aw-ruh^l hal soo eess-aw-yo
Korean do can

I don't speak Korean.
한국어를 못 해요.
hangugeoreul mot haeyo.
han-goog-aw-ruh^l mot eh-yo
Korean cannot do

To say *I speak ...*, there are two possibilities:
...를 할 수 있어요 **-reul hal su isseoyo** *I can speak ...* or simply
...를 해요 **-reul haeyo** *I speak ...*

I speak ...		
English.	영어 **yeongeo**	*yawng-aw*
Spanish.	스페인어 **seupeineo**	*suh-pay-een-aw*
French.	프랑스어 **peurangseueo**	*puh-rahng-suh-aw*
German.	독일어 **dogireo**	*tohg-eer-aw*
Italian.	이탈리아어 **italliaeo**	*ee-tal-lee-a-aw*
Japanese.	일본어 **ilboneo**	*eel-bon-aw*
Dutch.	네덜란드어 **nedeollandeueo**	*nay-dawl-lan-duh-aw*
	...를 해요 **...reul haeyo.**	*ruh^l heh-yo*

The name of a language is formed by adding 어 **-eo** after the name of the country, with the exception of English, which is 영어 **yeongeo**. (For the country names, see 'Saying where you're from'.)

I understand.	이해했어요. **ihaehaesseoyo**	*ee-eh-hess-aw-yo*
I don't understand.	모르겠어요. **moreugesseoyo**	*mo-ruh-gayss-aw-yo*
Pardon me?	뭐라고요? **mworagoyo**	*mwo-ra-go-yo*
Speak slowly, please.	천천히 말씀해 주세요. **cheoncheonhi malsseumhae juseyo**	*chawn-chawn-ee mal-ssum-eh choo-say-yo*

Could you repeat that?	다시 말씀해 주시겠어요? **dasi malsseumhae jusigesseoyo**	*ta-shee mal-ssum-eh choo-see-gayss-aw-yo*

I can't understand what you're saying.
무슨 말인지 모르겠어요.
museun marinji moreugesseoyo.
moo-sun mar-een-jee mo-ruh-gayss-aw-o
what word-if not-understand

Could you speak in English?
영어로 말씀해 주시겠어요?
yeongeoro malsseumhae jusigesseoyo?
yawng-aw-ro mal-ssum-eh choo-shi-gayss-aw-yo
English-in speak please

이거 **igeo** *this* is used to refer to something close, 그거 **geugeo** *that* when it is closer to the person being addressed, and 저거 **jeogeo** *that over there* when it is farther away.

How do I say this in Korean?	이거 한국어로 어떻게 말해요? **igeo hangugeoro eotteoke malhaeyo**	*ee-gaw han-goog-aw-ro aw-taw-kay mal-eh-yo*
that	그거 **geugeo**	*kuh-gaw*
that over there	저거 **jeogeo**	*chaw-gaw*

Meeting people

First meeting

The level of formality when meeting someone depends on the context. In professional situations, typically two people will start by exchanging business cards and then shake hands.

The card allows you to use the person's title to address them, using the honorific 님 **-nim** *sir, madam* after the title: e.g. 부장 **bujang** *director* becomes 부장님 **bujangnim**. The polite formal verb ending is used, which is ㅂ니다 **-mnida** (after a vowel) / 습니다 **-seumnida** (after a consonant) in statements, or ㅂ니까 **-mnikka** (after a vowel) / 습니까 **-seumnikka** (after a consonant) in questions.

Here is my business card.
여기 제 명함입니다.
yeogi je myeonghamimnida.
yaw-gee chay myawng-a-mim-nee-da
here my business-card-be

Director, sir/ma'am, I am honoured to meet you.
부장님, 만나뵙게 되어 영광입니다.
bujangnim, mannaboepge doeeo yeonggwangimnida.
boo-jahng-nim man-na-bway^{p}-kay dway-aw yawng-kahng-im-nee-da

Outside of work contexts, if you know someone, call them by their first name followed by the honorific suffix 씨 **ssi**. You can greet them with a slight bow (simply tilt the head forward).

It's nice to meet you, Carol.
캐롤 씨, 반가워요.
kaerol ssi, bangawoyo.
keh-rol shee, pahn-ga-wo-yo

Thank you for your welcome.
환영해 주셔서 감사해요.
hwanyeonghae jusyeoseo gamsahaeyo.
hwan-yawng-eh choo-syaw-saw kam-sa-eh-yo

Introducing yourself or someone else

Koreans introduce themselves giving their family name first, followed by their first name. For example, Ban Ki-moon (former Secretary General of the UN) should be addressed as Mr Ban: Ban is his family name and Ki-moon his given name. For Westerners, the order doesn't matter; you can introduce yourself by starting with either your family name or your first name.

I'm ...
...이에요/예요.
...ieyo/yeyo.
...ee-ay-yo/yay-yo

My name is ...
제 이름은 ...입니다.
je ireumeun ...imnida.
chay ee-ruh-muhn ...eem-nee-da

To introduce someone else, the honorific suffix 씨 **ssi** always follows the first name, except among friends or family. Avoid using it after the family name, as this could be interpreted as derogatory (except on the news or in newspapers). Note that this honorific suffix is never used to refer to oneself.

This is ...	이 분은 ... 씨예요. **i buneun ... ssiyeyo.**	*ee boon-uhn ...see-yay-yo*
my friend Carol.	제 친구 캐롤 **je chingu kaerol**	*chay chin-goo keh-rol*
my wife.	제 아내 **je anae**	*chay ah-neh*
my husband.	제 남편 **je nampyeon**	*chay nam-pyawn*

Saying where you're from

Where are you from?
어디에서 오셨어요?
eodieseo osyeosseoyo?
aw-dee-ay-saw o-shawss-aw-yo
where-from come

This question could refer either to your nationality or to the company you work for or school you go to.

I'm American.
미국에서 왔어요.
migugeseo wasseoyo.
mee-gook-ay-saw wass-aw-yo
United-States-from come

I'm Irish.
아일랜드에서 왔어요.
aillaendeueseo wasseoyo.
a-il-len-duh-ay-saw wass-aw-yo
Ireland-from come

I'm a student at the University of ...
...대학에서 왔어요
...daehageseo wasseoyo.
...teh-ag-ay-saw wass-aw-yo
...university-from come

Many (but not all) country names use the English terms pronounced in a Korean way. To form the nationality, just add 사람 **saram** *person* after the country.

Australia / Australian	호주 / 호주 사람 **hoju / hoju saram**	*ho-joo / ho-joo sa-ram*
Canada / Canadian	캐나다 / 캐나다 사람 **kaenada / kaenada saram**	*keh-na-da / keh-na-da sa-ram*
France / French	프랑스 / 프랑스 사람 **peurangseu / peurangseu saram**	*puh-rahng-suh / puh-rahng-suh sa-ram*
Germany / German	독일 / 독일 사람 **dogil / dogil saram**	*tohg-il / tohg-il sa-ram*
Ireland / Irish	아일랜드 / 아일랜드 사람 **aillaendeu / aillaendeu saram**	*a-il-len-duh / a-il-len-duh sa-ram*
Italy / Italian	이탈리아 / 이탈리아 사람 **itallia / itallia saram**	*ee-tal-lee-a / ee-tal-lee-a sa-ram*
Japan / Japanese	일본 / 일본 사람 **ilbon / ilbon saram**	*il-bon / il-bon sa-ram*

Mexico / Mexican	멕시코 / 멕시코 사람 **meksiko / meksiko saram**	*mek-shee-ko / mek-shee-ko sa-ram*
Netherlands / Dutch	네덜란드 / 네덜란드 사람 **nedeollandeu / nedeollandeu saram**	*nay-dawl-lan-duh / nay-dawl-lan-duh sa-ram*
New Zealand / New Zealander	뉴질랜드 / 뉴질랜드 사람 **nyujillaendeu/ nyujillaendeu saram**	*nyoo-jeel-len-duh / nyoo-jeel-len-duh sa-ram*
South Africa / South African	남아공 / 남아공 사람 **namagong / namagong saram**	*nam-a-gong / nam-a-gong sa-ram*
Spain / Spanish	스페인 / 스페인 사람 **seupein / seupein saram**	*suh-pay-in / suh-pay-in sa-ram*
United Kingdom / British	영국 / 영국 사람 **yeongguk / yeongguk saram**	*yawng-goo^k / yawng-goo^k sa-ram*
United States / American	미국 / 미국 사람 **miguk / miguk saram**	*mee-goo^k / mee-goo^k sa-ram*

Giving your age

Age is counted differently in Korea than in Western countries. When a baby is born, it is considered to be age 1 (rather than 0). Then it gains a year each 1 January (rather than on its birthday). So every Korean gets a year older on the first of the year. Personal birthdays are celebrated, but people don't add a year on that day.

Say a baby is born on 11 December: at birth, it's already 1 year old. A month later, on 1 January, it becomes 2 years old though it has only been alive less than a month! So if you're in Korea before your birthday, you have to add two years to your age; after your birthday, add one year. Don't worry – although you'll age while travelling in Korea, you'll get younger when you go back home!

Excuse me, how old are you?
실례지만, 나이가 어떻게 되세요?
sillyejiman, naiga eotteoke doeseyo?
shil-lay-jee-man na-ee-ga aw-ᴛaw-kay dway-say-yo
impoliteness-but, age how become

To give an age, the Korean number system is used:

I'm ...		
26 years old.	26 **seumul yeoseot**	*suh-mool yaw-saw^t*
10 / 11 / 12 years old.	열 **yeol /** 열 한 **yeol han /** 열 두 **yeol du**	*yawl / yawl han / yawl too*
20 / 30 / 40 years old.	스물 **seumul /** 서른 **seoreun /** 마흔 **maheun**	*suh-muhl / saw-ruhn / ma-huhn*
50 / 60 / 70 years old.	쉰 **swin /** 예순 **yesun /** 일흔 **ilheun**	*shin / yay-soon / il-uhn*
80 / 90 / 100 years old.	여든 **yeodeun /** 아흔 **aheun /** 백 **baek**	*yaw-duhn / a-huhn / pehk*
	...살이에요. **sarieyo.**	*sar-ee-ay-yo*

Talking about your family

In Korea, not only married people wear a wedding ring, but many unmarried couples as well. Traditionally, single people lived with their parents until they got married, and it was rare for unmarried couples to live together. Today, however, these customs are changing.

Are you married?
결혼하셨어요?
gyeolhonhasyeosseoyo?
kyawl-on-ha-shyawss-aw-yo
be-married

Yes, I'm married.
네, 결혼했어요.
ne, gyeolhonhaesseoyo.
nay kyawl-on-ess-aw-yo
yes, be-married

No, I'm single.
아니요, 미혼이에요.
aniyo, mihonieyo.
a-nee-yo mee-hohn-ee-ay-yo
no, single-be

wife	부인 **buin** (formal) **/** 아내 **anae**	*poo-in / a-neh*
husband	남편 **nampyeon**	*nam-pyawn*
girlfriend	여자 친구 **yeoja chingu**	*yaw-ja chin-goo*
boyfriend	남자 친구 **namja chingu**	*nam-ja chin-goo*

The terms for family members in Korea are a bit more specific than in English, indicating whether a grandparent is on the mother's or father's side or a sibling is older or younger. In addition, males use the terms 누나 **nuna** *older sister* and 형 **hyeong** *older brother*, while females use 언니 **eonni** *older sister* and 오빠 **oppa** *older brother*. The latter can be used to refer to an older man in an affectionate way.

I (f.) *have an older sister and a younger brother.*
언니하고 남동생이 있어요.
eonnihago namdongsaengi isseoyo.
awn-nee-a-go nam-dong-seng-ee eess-aw-yo
older-sister-and younger-brother have

family	가족 **gajok**	*ka-jo*ᵏ
parents	부모님 **bumonim**	*poo-mo-nim*
mother / mum	어머니 **eomeoni /** 엄마 **eomma**	*aw-maw-nee / awm-ma*
father / dad	아버지 **abeoji /** 아빠 **appa**	*a-baw-chee / a-*ᴘ*a*

daughter	딸 **ttal**	*Tal*
son	아들 **adeul**	*a-duhl*
older sister / older brother (of a female)	언니 **eonni /** 오빠 **oppa**	*awn-nee / o-Pa*
older sister / older brother (of a male)	누나 **nuna /** 형 **hyeong**	*noo-na / hawng*
younger sister	여동생 **yeodongsaeng**	*yaw-dong-seng*
younger brother	남동생 **namdongsaeng**	*nam-dong-seng*
grandmother (paternal) / *grandmother* (maternal)	할머니 **halmeoni /** 외할머니 **oehalmeoni**	*hal-maw-nee / way-al-maw-nee*
grandfather (paternal) / *grandfather* (maternal)	할아버지 **harabeoji /** 외할아버지 **oeharabeoji**	*har-a-baw-jee / way-ar-a-baw-jee*

In-laws and step-parents also have specific terms:

mother-/father-in-law (husband's parents)	시어머니 **sieomeoni** / 시아버지 **siabeoji**	*shee-aw-maw-nee / shee-a-baw-chee*
mother-/father-in-law (wife's parents)	장모님 **jangmonim** / 장인어른 **jangineoreun**	*chang-mo-nim / chang-een-aw-run*
stepmother (polite) / (informal)	새어머니 **saeeomeoni**/ 새엄마 **saeeomma**	*seh-aw-maw-nee / seh-awm-ma*
stepfather (polite) / (informal)	새아버지 **saeabeoji** / 새아빠 **saeappa**	*seh-a-baw-jee / seh-a-Pa*

Saying what you do

When asked about their job, Koreans will often reply first with whether they are an employer, an employee or a civil servant before specifying the name of the company or profession.

What do you do?
무슨 일 하세요?
museun il haseyo?
moo-suhn il ha-say-yo
what work do

What's your profession?
직업이 어떻게 되세요?
jigeobi eotteoke doeseyo?
cheek-awb-ee aw-Taw-kay day-say-yo
job how become

I'm an employee.
회사원이에요.
hoesawonieyo.
hway-sa-wohn-ee-ay-yo
employee-be

I work at ...
... 에서 일해요.
...eseo ilhaeyo.
ay-saw il-eh-yo
... at work

I'm (a/an) ...		
artist.	예술가 **yesulga**	*yay-sool-ga*
bank employee.	은행원 **eunhaengwon**	*uhn-eng-won*
civil servant / public sector employee.	공무원 **gongmuwon**	*kong-moo-won*
cook.	요리사 **yorisa**	*yo-ree-sa*
doctor.	의사 **uisa**	*wee-sa*
engineer.	엔지니어 **enjinieo**	*en-jee-nee-aw*
housewife.	가정주부 **gajeongjubu**	*ka-jawng-joo-boo*
job seeker.	구직자 **gujikja**	*koo-jik-ja*
lawyer.	변호사 **byeonhosa**	*pyawn-o-sa*
professor.	교수 **gyosu**	*kyo-soo*
retiree.	퇴직자 **toejikja**	*tay-jik-ja*
teacher.	선생님 **seonsaengnim**	*sawn-seng-nim*
	...이에요/예요. **ieyo / yeyo.**	*ee-ay-yo / yay-yo*

To talk about a school one goes to, the verb 다니다 **danida** *to attend* is often used, followed by the name of the establishment.

I go to ...		
lower secondary school.	중학교 **junghakgyo**	*choong-ha^k-kyo*
upper secondary school.	고등학교 **godeunghakgyo**	*go-dung-ha^k-kyo*
university.	대학교 **daehakgyo**	*teh-ha^k-kyo*
	...에 다녀요. **e danyeoyo.**	*ay ta-nyaw-yo*

I'm studying ...		
architecture.	건축학 **geonchukak**	*kawn-chook-hag*
biology.	생물학 **saengmulhak**	*seng-mool-hag*
business administration.	경영학 **gyeongyeonghak**	*kyawng-yawng-hag*
computer science.	컴퓨터 공학 **keompyuteo gonghak**	*kawm-pyoo-taw kong-hag*
economics.	경제학 **gyeongjehak**	*kyawng-jay-hag*
history.	역사학 **yeoksahak**	*yawk-sa-hag*
literature.	문학 **munhak**	*moon-hag*
medicine.	의학 **uihak**	*wee-hag*
psychology.	심리학 **simrihak**	*shim-nee-hag*
	...을 공부해요. **eul gongbuhaeyo.**	*uhl kong-boo-heh-yo*

Religion and traditions

The main religions in Korea today are Buddhism, Catholicism and Protestantism. Korean society is traditionally based on Confucian teachings, which emphasize 예의 **yeui** *politeness* and 존중 **jonjung** *respect* towards others, especially the elderly. It is polite to offer your seat to seniors on buses, metros, etc.

Please sit here.
여기 앉으세요.
yeogi anjeuseyo.
yaw-gee anj-uh-say-yo
here sit-down

You are very polite!
예의바른 사람이군요.
yeuibareun saramigunyo.
yay-wee-ba-ruhn sa-ram-ee-goon-yo
be-polite person-be

What is your religion?
종교가 어떻게 되세요?
jonggyoga eotteoke doeseyo?
chong-gyo-ga aw-taw-kay day-say-yo
religion how be

I'm (a/an) ...		
atheist.	무교 / 무종교 **mugyo / mujonggyo**	*moo-gyo / moo-jong-gyo*
Buddhist.	불교 신자 **bulgyo sinja**	*pool-gyo sheen-ja*
Catholic.	가톨릭교 신자 **gatollikgyo sinja**	*ka-tol-lik-gyo sheen-ja*
Jewish.	유태교 신자 **yutaegyo sinja**	*yoo-teh-gyo sheen-ja*
Muslim.	이슬람 신자 **iseullam sinja**	*ee-suhl-lam sheen-ja*
Protestant.	기독교 신자 **gidokgyo sinja**	*gee-dok-gyo sheen-ja*
	...예요. **yeyo.**	*yay-yo*

The weather

Korea has a temperate climate with four distinct 계절 **gyejeol** *seasons*: 봄 **bom** *spring*, 여름 **yeoreum** *summer*, 가을 **gaeul** *autumn*, 겨울 **gyeoul** *winter*. Generally, spring and autumn are mild and pleasant, summer is hot and humid, and winter is often very dry and cold. The summer can bring typhoons, so watch the 일기 예보 **ilgi yebo** *weather forecast*!

What's the weather forecast for this weekend?
이번 주말 일기예보가 어때요?
ibeon jumal ilgiyeboga eottaeyo?
ee-bawn choo-mal il-gee-ay-bo-ga aw-Teh-yo
this weekend weather-forecast be-how

It's ... ('weather')	날씨가... **nalssiga**	*nal-shee-ga*
nice.	좋아요. **joayo**	*cho-a-yo*
hot.	더워요. **deowoyo**	*taw-wo-yo*
warm / mild.	따뜻해요. **ttatteutaeyo**	*Ta-Tuht-eh-yo*
cool.	시원해요. **siwonhaeyo**	*shee-won-eh-yo*

cold.	추워요. **chuwoyo**	*choo-wo-yo*
humid.	습해요. **seupaeyo**	*suhp-eh-yo*
dry.	건조해요. **geonjohaeyo**	*kawn-jo-eh-yo*

The sky is clear.	하늘이 맑아요. **haneuri malgayo**	*ha-nuhr-ee mal-ga-yo*
It's snowing.	눈이 와요. **nuni wayo**	*noon-ee wa-yo*
It's raining.	비가 와요. **biga wayo**	*pee-ga wa-yo*
It's windy.	바람이 불어요. **barami bureoyo**	*pa-rahm-ee poor-aw-yo*
It's cloudy.	구름이 끼었어요. **gureumi kkieosseoyo**	*koo-ruhm-ee кee-awss-aw-yo*
There's a typhoon coming.	태풍이 와요. **taepungi wayo**	*teh-poong-ee wa-yo*
It's foggy.	안개가 끼었어요. **angaega kkieosseoyo**	*an-geh-ga кee-awss-aw-yo*
umbrella	우산 **usan**	*oo-san*

Expressing opinions and likes/dislikes

To avoid making people feel uncomfortable, Koreans don't usually express their dissatisfaction, except in shops, etc.

That's fine. ('be-good / all-right')	좋아요 / 괜찮아요. **joayo / gwaenchanayo**	*cho-a-yo / kwen-chan-a-yo*
It's comfortable.	편해요. **pyeonhaeyo**	*pyawn-eh-yo*
It's not comfortable.	불편해요. **bulpyeonhaeyo**	*pool-pyawn-heh-yo*
It's unpleasant.	불쾌해요. **bulkwaehaeyo**	*pool-keh-eh-yo*
It's regrettable.	유감이에요. **yugamieyo**	*yoo-gam-ee-ay-yo*
It's interesting / funny.	재미있어요. **jaemiisseoyo**	*cheh-mee-eess-aw-yo*
It's not very good.	별로예요. **byeolloyeyo**	*pyawl-lo-ay-yo*

It's a little difficult for me.	조금 곤란해요. **jogeum gollanhaeyo**	*cho-guhm kol-lan-eh-yo*
It annoys me.	짜증나요. **jjajeungnayo**	*CHa-jung-na-yo*
It's boring.	심심해요. **simsimhaeyo**	*shim-shim-eh-yo*
I like it.	마음에 들어요. **maeume deureoyo**	*ma-uhm-ay tuhr-aw-yo*
I don't like it.	마음에 안 들어요. **maeume an deureoyo**	*ma-uhm-ay an duhr-aw-yo*
It's OK / not bad / so-so.	그냥 그래요. **geunyang geuraeyo**	*kuh-nyang kuh-reh-yo*
I'm not sure.	잘 모르겠어요. **jal moreugesseoyo**	*chal mo-ruh-gayss-aw-yo*

Invitations

It's rare for Koreans to invite people over. Usually they go out somewhere to meet up.

Shall we go ...		
to the park?	공원에 **gongwone**	*kong-won-ay*
for a drink?	술 마시러 **sul masireo**	*sool ma-shee-raw*
to a bar?	바에 **bae**	*pa-ay*
to a restaurant?	식당에 **sikdange**	*shik-tang-ay*
to a café?	커피숍에 **keopisyobe**	*kaw-pee-shop-ay*
for a meal? / to eat out?	밥 먹으러 **bap meogeureo**	*pa^{p} mawg-uh-raw*
to a film?	영화보러 **yeonghwaboreo**	*yawng-wa-bo-raw*
to a show?	공연보러 **gongyeonboreo**	*kong-yawn-bo-raw*
to a karaoke box?	노래방에 **noraebange***	*no-reh-bang-ay*
	...갈까요? **galkkayo?**	*kal-Ka-yo*

* Literally, 노래 **norae** *song* and 방 **bang** *room*.

Great!
좋아요.
joayo.
cho-a-yo

Yes, let's go!
네, 가요.
ne, gayo.
nay ka-yo

I don't want to.
싫은데요.
sireundeyo.
shir-uhn-day-yo

If you have to refuse an invitation, it's best to be indirect:

I'm sorry, but I have something else planned.
죄송하지만 다른 약속이 있어요.
joesonghajiman dareun yaksogi isseoyo.
chway-song-a-chi-man ta-ruhn yak-sog-ee eess-aw-yo
sorry-but other appointment have

I'm sorry, I'll come next time.
죄송하지만 다음에 가요.
joesonghajiman daeume gayo.
chway-song-a-jee-man ta-uhm-ay ga-yo
sorry-but next-time go

If you are invited to a Korean home, remove your shoes before entering. They will be kept near the door so you can easily put them back on when you leave.

Thank you for inviting me.
초대해 주셔서 감사해요.
chodaehae jusyeoseo gamsahaeyo.
cho-deh-eh joo-shyaw-saw kam-sa-eh-yo
invite because thank-you

Make yourself at home.
편하게 하세요.
pyeonhage haseyo.
pyawn-a-gay ha-say-yo
ease have

Don't be taken aback if your host compliments you on your physical appearance – this is common in Korea. Just return the compliment!

You are really tall! (to a man)
키가 정말 크시네요!
kiga jeongmal keusineyo!
kee-ga chawng-mal kuh-shee-nay-o
height really be-tall

You are beautiful! (to a woman)
미인이시네요!
miinisineyo!
mee-een-ee-shee-nay-o
beautiful-woman-be

You give a good impression!
인상이 좋으시네요.
insangi joeusineyo.
in-sang-ee cho-uh-shee-nay-o
impression be-good

You look so young!
나이보다 젊어 보이세요.
naiboda jeolmeo boiseyo.
na-ee-bo-da chawlm-aw bo-ee-say-o
age young seem

At the table, your host will humbly invite you to eat ('I haven't prepared much, but enjoy'). When offered food, it is impolite to refuse. If there are elderly people at the table, don't start eating until they begin their meal.

Equally, Koreans don't smoke or drink alcohol directly in front of an older person; a younger person turns his or her head to the side to drink.

Enjoy your meal! (wish offered by the host)
차린 건 없지만 맛있게 드세요.
charin geon eopjiman masitge deuseyo.
cha-reen gawn aw^{p}-chee-man mash-ee^{t}-kay duh-say-yo
prepare thing nothing-but deliciously eat

I will enjoy it! (thanks offered by the guest)
잘 먹겠습니다.
jal meokgetseumnida.
chal maw^{k}-ke^{t}-suhm-nee-da
well will-eat

It's really delicious!
정말 맛있네요!
jeongmal masinneyo!
chawng-mal mash-een-nay-yo

Bottoms up!
원 샷! **won syat!**
won sha^t

Cheers!
건배! **geonbae!**
kawn-beh

Meeting up …

Koreans often suggest meeting up with 제가 밥 살게요 **jega bap salgeyo** *[chay-ga pa^p sal-kay-yo]* *Let me treat you to a meal.* or 밥 사 주세요 **bap sa juseyo** *[pa^p sa joo-say-yo]* *Treat me to a meal.* Then you just arrange the time and place.

What time / Where shall we meet?
몇 시에 /어디에서 만날까요?
myeot sie / eodieseo mannalkkayo?
myaw^t shee-ay / aw-dee-ay-saw man-na^l-Ka-yo
what time / where meet

I'll wait for you at the exit of the metro.
지하철 출구 앞에서 기다릴게요.
jihacheol chulgu apeseo gidarilgeyo.
chee-a-chawl chool-goo ap-ay-saw kee-da-ree^l-kay-yo
metro exit in-front-of wait

at the side / next to	옆 **yeop**	*yaw^p*
front / back	앞 **ap** / 뒤 **dwi**	*a^p / tee*
left side / right side	왼쪽 **oenjjok** / 오른쪽 **oreunjjok**	*wen-CHO^k / o-ruhn-CHO^k*
inside / outside	안 **an** / 밖 **bak**	*an / pa^k*

... and chatting up

In Korea, being polite and respectful increases your chance of success in romancing someone.

Do you have a moment?
시간 있으세요?
sigan isseuseyo?
shee-gan eess-uh-say-o
time have

How do you feel about me?
저를 어떻게 생각하세요?
jeoreul eotteoke saenggakaseyo?
chaw-ruhl aw-TAW-kay seng-gak-a-say-o
me how think

I like you.
그 쪽이 마음에 들어요.
geu jjogi maeume deureoyo.
kuh CHOK-ee ma-uhm-ay tuhr-aw-yo

Can I have your phone number?
전화번호 좀 알 수 있을까요?
jeonhwabeonho jom al su isseulkkayo?
chawn-hwa-bawn-ho jom al soo eess-uhl-KA-yo

Can we go for a coffee?
커피 한 잔 할까요?
keopi han jan halkkayo?
kaw-pee han jan hal-KA-yo
coffee a cup do

Time and the calendar

Telling the time

Both the Korean and Sino-Korean number systems (see Days 12 and 13 and the front cover flap) are used to give the time: the former for the hour and the latter for the minutes. The time is often preceded by the time of day being referred to: 오전 **ojeon** *morning, a.m.* or 오후 **ohu** *afternoon, p.m.*

What time is it?
몇 시예요?
myeot siyeyo?
myaw^{t} shee-yay-yo
what time-be

It's 2:40 p.m.
오후 2 시 40분이에요.
ohu du si sasip bunieyo.
o-hoo too shee sa-shee^{p} poon-ee-ay-yo
afternoon 2 hour 40 minute-be

time / hour / o'clock	시 **si**	*shee*
minute	분 **bun**	*poon*
morning	오전 **ojeon**	*o-jun*
noon / midday	정오 **jeongo**	*chawng-o*
afternoon	오후 **ohu**	*o-hoo*
evening	저녁 **jeonyeok**	*chaw-nyaw^{k}*
night	밤 **bam**	*pam*
dawn	새벽 **saebyeok**	*seh-byaw^{k}*
sunset	해질녘 **haejillyeok**	*heh-jeel-lyaw^{k}*

1:00	한 시 **han si**	*han shee*	*7:00*	일곱 시 **ilgop si**	*il-go^{p} shee*
2:00	두 시 **du si**	*too shee*	*8:00*	여덟 시 **yeodeol si**	*yaw-dawl shee*
3:00	세 시 **se si**	*say shee*	*9:00*	아홉 시 **ahop si**	*a-ho^{p} shee*
4:00	네 시 **ne si**	*nay shee*	*10:00*	열 시 **yeol si**	*yawl shee*
5:00	다섯 시 **daseot si**	*ta-saw^{t} shee*	*11:00*	열한 시 **yeolhan si**	*yawl han shee*
6:00	여섯 시 **yeoseot si**	*yaw-saw^{t} shee*	*12:00*	열두 시 **yeoldu si**	*yawl too shee*

Dates, days, months and seasons

The order of a date goes from the largest to the smallest unit of time, i.e. year, month, day.

Sino-Korean numbers are used.

What is the date?
오늘이 몇 월 며칠이에요?
oneuri myeot wol myeochirieyo?
o-nuhr-ee myaw^{t} wol myaw-cheer-ee-ay-o
today what month what-day-be

It's the 30th of August.
8월 30일이에요.
par wol samsib irieyo.
par ol sam-sheeb eer-ee-ay-o
8 month 30 be

What's today's date?
오늘이 며칠이에요?
oneuri myeochirieyo?
o-nuhr-ee myaw-cheer-ee-ay-o
today what-day-be

Today is the 28th.
28 일이에요.
isippar irieyo.
ee-shee^{p}-par eer-ee-ay-o
28 be

Days of the week

It's ...		
Monday.	월요일 **woryoil**	*wor-yo-ee^{l}*
Tuesday.	화요일 **hwayoil**	*hwa-yo-ee^{l}*
Wednesday.	수요일 **suyoil**	*soo-yo-ee^{l}*
Thursday.	목요일 **mogyoil**	*mog-yo-ee^{l}*
Friday.	금요일 **geumyoil**	*kuhm-yo-ee^{l}*
Saturday.	토요일 **toyoil**	*toh-yo-ee^{l}*
Sunday.	일요일 **iryoil**	*eer-yo-ee^{l}*
	...이에요. **ieyo.**	*ee-ay-yo*

Months of the year

What month is it?
몇 월이에요?
myeot worieyo?
myawt wor-ee-ay-yo

It's July.
7월이에요.
chir worieyo.
cheer wor-ee-ay-yo

January	1월 **irwol**	*eer-wol*
February	2월 **iwol**	*ee-wol*
March	3월 **samwol**	*sam-wol*
April	4월 **sawol**	*sa-wol*
May	5월 **owol**	*oh-wol*
June	6월 **yuwol**	*yoo-wol*
July	7월 **chirwol**	*cheer-wol*
August	8월 **parwol**	*par-wol*
September	9월 **guwol**	*koo-wol*
October	10월 **siwol**	*shee-wol*
November	11월 **sibirwol**	*sheeb-eer-wol*
December	12월 **sibiwol**	*sheeb-ee-wol*

Seasons

spring	봄 **bom**	*pohm*
summer	여름 **yeoreum**	*yaw-ruhm*
autumn	가을 **gaeul**	*ka-uhl*
winter	겨울 **gyeoul**	*kyo-uhl*

Talking about 'when'

When did you arrive in Korea?
언제 한국에 도착하셨어요?
eonje hanguge dochakasyeosseoyo?
awn-jay han-gook-ay do-chak-a-shyoss-aw-yo
when Korea-in arrive

Last month.
지난달에요.
jinandareyo.
chee-nan-dar-ay-yo
last-month-in

yesterday	어제 **eoje**	*aw-jay*
the day before	전날 **jeonnal**	*chawn-nal*
this week	이번 주 **ibeon ju**	*ee-bawn choo*
last week	지난주 **jinanju**	*chee-nan-joo*
this month	이번 달 **ibeon dal**	*ee-bawn tal*
last month	지난달 **jinandal**	*chee-nan-dal*

To express duration:

for 2 years	이* 년 동안 **i nyeon dongan**	*ee nyawn tong-an*
for 2 months	두** 달 동안 **du dal dongan**	*too dal tong-an*
for 2 weeks	이* 주 동안 **i ju dongan**	*ee joo tong-an*
for 2 days	이* 일 동안 **i il dongan**	*ee eel tong-an*
for 2 hours	두** 시간 동안 **du sigan dongan**	*too shee-gan tong-an*

* Sino-Korean number ** Korean number

How long are you staying in Korea?
얼마 동안 한국에 머물어요?
eolma dongan hanguge meomureoyo?
awl-ma tong-an han-goog-ay maw-mool-aw-yo
how-long for Korea-in stay

I'm staying for 15 days.
15일 동안 머물어요. **sibo il dongan meomureoyo.**
shee-bo eel tong-an maw-mool-aw-yo
15 day for stay

I've been studying Korean for two years.
2년 동안 한국어를 공부했어요.
i nyeon dongan hangugeoreul gongbuhaesseoyo.
ee nyawn tong-an han-gook-aw-ruhl kong-boo-ehss-aw-yo
2 year for Korean study

Festivals and holidays

Traditionally, Korea used the lunar calendar (음력 **eumnyeok**) rather than the solar calendar (양력 **yangnyeok**), so it still celebrates certain lunar festivals, whose date varies each year. For example, though both are holidays, the Lunar New Year is more important than 1 January in Korea.

On the new moon of the first lunar month of the year, families hold a ceremony for ancestors (called a 차례 **charye**) wearing traditional Korean clothing (한복 **hanbok**). Younger family members make a New Year's bow (세배 **sebae**) to their elders, who give them gifts of money (세뱃돈 **sebaetdon**) and good wishes for the future. The morning meal is rice-cake soup (떡국 **tteokguk**). It is said that each bowl adds an extra year to one's life, so children eat several bowls! The Lunar New Year is virtually the only time when all public services and shops are closed.

The autumn harvest festival (추석 **chuseok**) is celebrated on the full moon of the eighth lunar month (in September or October). For this festival, families also hold a 차례 **charye** and wear 한복 **hanbok**, and one of the side dishes of the meal is rice cakes that are stuffed with red bean paste (송편 **songpyeon**) and steamed over pine needles. Buddha's Birthday is also commemorated according to the lunar calendar; the occasion is celebrated with the spectacular Lotus Lantern Festival.

What is the traditional dish for the Lunar New Year?
설날에 무슨 음식을 먹어요?
seollare museun eumsigeul meogeoyo?
sawl-lar-ay moo-suhn uhm-sheek-uhl mawk-aw-yo
lunar-new-year-on what food eat

Happy New Year!
새해 복 많이 받으세요!
saehae bok mani badeuseyo!
seh-eh bo[k] man-ee bad-uh-say-yo
new-year happiness much receive

New Year's Day (1 Jan)	신정 **sinjeong**	*sheen-jawng*
Lunar New Year (Jan or Feb)	설날 **seollal /** 구정 **gujeong**	*sawl-lal / koo-jawng*
Buddha's Birthday (April or May)	석가탄신일 **seokgatansinil**	*sawk-ka-tan-sheen-il*
Parents' Day (8 May)	어버이날 **eobeoinal**	*aw-baw-ee-nal*
National Liberation Day (15 Aug)	광복절 **gwangbokjeol**	*kwang-bo[k]-chawl*
Harvest Festival (Sept or Oct)	한가위 **hangawi /** 추석 **chuseok**	*han-ga-wee / choo-saw[k]*
National Foundation Day (3 Oct)	개천절 **gaecheonjeol**	*keh-chawn-jawl*
Hangeul Day (9 Oct)	한글날 **hangeullal**	*han-guhl-lal*
Christmas (25 Dec)	크리스마스 **keuriseumaseu**	*kuh-ree-suh-ma-s*

Asking for assistance

Emergencies

Hopefully, you won't need this information, but in case of a medical emergency, fire or accident, call 119.

Help! ('rescue')
사람 살려!
saram sallyeo!
sa-ram sal-lyaw
person save

Help me!
도와 주세요!
dowa juseyo!
toh-wa joo-say-yo
help please

Fire!
불이야!
buriya!
poor-ee-ya
fire-be

I'm lost.
길을 잃어버렸어요.
gireul ireobeoryeosseoyo.
keer-ul eer-aw-baw-ross-aw-yo
path lose

I don't feel very well.
몸이 안 좋아요.
momi an joayo.
mohm-ee an jo-a-yo
body not be-well

Call a doctor, please!
의사를 불러 주세요.
uisareul bulleo juseyo.
wee-sa-ruhl puhl-law joo-say-o
doctor call please

Call 119, please!
119를 불러 주세요.
irilgureul bulleo juseyo.
eel-il-goo-ruhl puhl-law joo-say-o
119 call please

There has been a car accident.
교통사고가 났어요. **gyotongsagoga nasseoyo.**
kyo-tong-sa-go-ga nass-aw-yo
car-accident happen

ambulance	앰뷸런스 **aembyulleonseu**	*em-byool-lawn-s*
health insurance	의료 보험 **uiryo boheom**	*way-ryo po-hawm*

Loss and theft

To report a crime, call 112.

Take me to the police station, please. ('police-station-to take...')
경찰서에 데려다 주세요.
gyeongchalseoe deryeoda juseyo.
kyawng-chal-saw-ay tay-ryaw-da choo-say-o

I've lost my passport. ('passport lose')
여권을 잃어버렸어요.
yeogwoneul ireobeoryeosseoyo.
yaw-kwon-ul eer-aw-baw-ryoss-aw-yo

My wallet has been stolen.
지갑을 도둑맞았어요.
jigabeul dodungmajasseoyo.
chee-gab-ul to-doong-maj-ass-aw-o
wallet be-stolen

Could you call someone who speaks English?
영어 하는 사람을 불러 주세요.
yeongeo haneun sarameul bulleo juseyo.
yawng-aw ha-nun sa-ram-uhl pool-law choo-say-yo
English do person call please

interpreter	통역사 **tongyeoksa**	*tong-yawk-sa*
translator	번역가 **beonyeokga**	*pawn-yawk-ga*

British / Irish / United States / Australian / South African / New Zealand Embassy	영국 **yeongguk /** 아일랜드 **aillaendeu /** 미국 **miguk /** 호주 **hoju /** 남아프리카 공화국 **namapeurika gonghwaguk /** 뉴질랜드 **nyujillaendeu** 대사관 **daesagwan**	*yawng-goo^k / a-il-len-duh / mee-goo^k / ho-joo / nam-a-puh-ree-ka kong-hwa-goo^k / nyoo-jeel-len-duh teh-sa-gwan*
airline ticket	비행기 표 **bihaenggi pyo**	*pee-eng-kee pyo*
bag	가방 **gabang**	*ka-bang*
camera	카메라 **kamera /** 사진기 **sajingi**	*ka-may-ra / sa-jin-kee*
computer	컴퓨터 **keompyuteo**	*kawm-pyoo-taw*
credit card / debit card	신용카드 **sinyongkadeu /** 직불카드 **jikbulkadeu**	*sheen-yong-ka-duh / chik-bool-ka-duh*

key	열쇠 **yeolsoe**	*yawl-say*
mobile phone	휴대 전화 **hyudae jeonhwa** / 핸드폰 **haendeupon**	*hyoo-deh jawn-hwa / hen-duh-pon*
money	돈 **don**	*ton*
ring	반지 **banji**	*pan-jee*

Signs and notices

금지 **geumji** means *prohibited*. Take note if you see this!

Danger	위험 **wiheom**	*wee-hawm*
Do not run	뛰지 마세요. **ttwiji maseyo**	*ᴛwee-jee ma-say-yo*
Do not touch	만지지 마세요. **manjiji maseyo**	*man-jee-jee ma-say-yo*
Emergency exit	비상구 **bisanggu**	*pee-sahng-goo*
Entrance / Exit	입구 **ipgu** / 출구 **chulgu**	*eep-goo / chool-goo*
Men / Women	남(성) **nam (seong)** / 여(성) **yeo (seong)**	*nam (sawng) / yaw (sawng)*
No access	접근 금지 **jeopgeun geumji**	*chawp-kuhn kuhm-jee*
No entry	출입 금지 **churip geumji**	*choor-ee^{p} kuhm-jee*
No parking	주차 금지 **jucha geumji**	*choo-cha kuhm-jee*
No smoking	금연 **geumyeon**	*kuhm-yawn*
No speeding	과속 금지 **gwasok geumji**	*kwa-so^{k} kuhm-jee*
No swimming	수영 금지 **suyeong geumji**	*soo-yawng kuhm-jee*
No thoroughfare / Road closed	통행 금지 **tonghaeng geumji**	*tong-heng kuhm-jee*
Open / Closed	열림 **yeollim** / 닫힘 **dachim**	*yawl-leem / ta^{t}-chim*
Toilets / Restroom	화장실 **hwajangsil**	*hwa-jahng-shil*

Travelling

There are various reasons you might have for visiting Korea.

Why have you come to Korea?
왜 한국에 오셨어요?
wae hanguge osyeosseoyo?
weh han-goog-ay o-syawss-aw-yo
why Korea-to come

Because I like K-drama. (Korean televised dramas)
한국 드라마를 좋아해서요.
hanguk deuramareul joahaeseoyo.
han-goo^k tuh-ra-ma-ruhl cho-a-eh-saw-yo
Korea drama like-because

Because my girlfriend/boyfriend is Korean.
여자 친구가 / 남자 친구가 한국 사람이라서요.
yeoja chinguga / namja chinguga hanguk saramiraseoyo.
yaw-ja chin-goo-ga / nam-ja chin-goo-ga han-goo^k sa-ram-ee-ra-saw-yo
female friend / male friend Korea person-be-because

I like ... very much.		
Korean food	한국 음식 **hanguk eumsik**	*han-goo^k um-shi^k*
Korean culture	한국 문화 **hanguk munhwa**	*han-goo^k moon-a*
hapkido (martial art)	합기도 **hapgido**	*hap-kee-doh*
K-pop	케이팝 **keipap**	*kay-ee-pap*
the Korean language	한국어 **hangugeo**	*han-goog-aw*
taekwondo	태권도 **taegwondo**	*teh-kon-doh*
	...을 **eul** / 를 **reul** 정말 좋아해요. **jeongmal joahaeyo.**	*uhl / ruhl* *chawng-mal* *cho-a-eh-yo*

Passport control and customs

For official interactions, use polite formal address.

Have you completed the customs declaration?
세관 신고서 작성하셨습니까?
segwan singoseo jakseonghasyeotseumnikka?
say-gwan shin-go-saw chak-sawng-a-shass-uhm-nee-κa
customs declaration write

Do you have anything to declare?
세관 신고할 물품이 있으십니까?
segwan singohal mulpumi isseusimnikka?
say-gwan shin-go-al mool-poom-ee eess-uh-sheem-nee-ka
customs declare objects have

Where have you come from?
어디에서 오십니까?
eodieseo osimnikka?
aw-dee-ay-saw o-sheem-nee-κa
where-from come

Passport, please.
여권을 보여 주십시오.
yeogwoneul boyeo jusipsio.
yaw-kwon-uhl po-yaw joo-ship-shi-o
passport show please

Where are you staying?
어디에서 머무르십니까?
eodieseo meomureusimnikka?
aw-dee-ay-saw maw-moo-ruh-sheem-nee-κa
where-in stay

Please take out your laptop.
컴퓨터를 꺼내 주십시오.
keompyuteoreul kkeonae jusipsio.
kawm-pyoo-taw-ruhl κaw-neh joo-ship-shi-o
laptop unpack please

Please remove your belt and your shoes.
벨트와 신발을 벗어 주십시오.
belteuwa sinbareul beoseo jusipsio.
pel-tuh-wa shin-bar-uhl poss-aw joo-shi^p-shi-o
belt-and shoes remove please

Would you please open your bag?
가방 안을 보여 주시겠습니까?
gabang aneul boyeo jusigetseumnikka?
ka-bang an-uhl po-yaw choo-shi-kay^t-suhm-nee-ĸa
bag inside show would-you-please

How long will you be staying in Korea?
한국에 얼마나 머무르십니까?
hanguge eolmana meomureusimnikka?
han-goog-ay awl-ma-na maw-moo-ruh-shim-nee-ĸa
Korea-in how-long stay

customs / customs declaration	세관 **segwan** / 세관 신고 **segwan singo**	*say-gwan / say-gwan shin-go*
customs clearance / customs duty	통관 **tonggwan** / 통관세 **tonggwanse**	*tong-gwan / tong-gwan-say*
duty-free shop	면세점 **myeonsejeom**	*myawn-say-jawm*
receipt	영수증 **yeongsujeung**	*yawng-soo-jung*

When you enter Korea, you will need to fill in an arrival card. The order of the information appears as follows:

family name	성 **seong**	*sawng*
first name	이름 **ireum**	*ee-ruhm*
sex: male / female	성별: 남 / 여 **seongbyeol: nam / yeo**	*sawng-byawl: nam / yaw*

nationality	국적 **gukjeok**	*goo^k-chaw^k*
date of birth	생년월일 **saengnyeonworil**	*seng-nyawn-wor-il*
passport number	여권 번호 **yeogwon beonho**	*yaw-gwon pawn-o*
residential address	거주국 주소 **geojuguk juso**	*kaw-joo-goo^k choo-so*
address in Korea	한국 주소 **hanguk juso**	*han-goo^k choo-so*
profession	직업 **jigeop**	*cheeg-aw^p*
purpose of trip	여행 목적 **yeohaeng mokjeok**	*yaw-heng mo^k-chaw^k*
flight number	비행 번호 **bihaeng beonho**	*pee-heng pawn-o*
gate number	게이트 번호 **geiteu beonho**	*kay-ee-tuh pawn-o*
signature	서명 **seomyeong**	*saw-myawng*

You may need to explain the purpose of your visit:

I've come ...		
to study.	공부하러 **gongbuhareo**	*kong-boo-a-raw*
to visit my family.	가족을 만나러 **gajogeul mannareo**	*ka-jog-uhl man-na-raw*
on business.	일 때문에 **il ttaemune**	*eel ᴛeh-moon-ay*
for travel.	여행하러 **yeohaenghareo**	*yaw-heng-a-raw*
	...왔어요. **wasseoyo.**	*wass-aw-yo*

Money

The Korean currency is called the 원 **won** (₩). Most businesses accept credit cards, but it's a good idea to have some cash as well. You can change money at the airport or in bureaux de change in cities–you will need to show ID for large amounts.

Where is a currency exchange?
환전소가 어디에 있어요?
hwanjeonsoga eodie isseoyo?
hwan-jawn-so-ga aw-dee-ay eess-aw-yo
currency-exchange-office where-at be-located

I'd like to exchange dollars/pounds for wons.
달러/파운드를 원화로 환전해 주세요.
dalleo/paundeureul wonhwaro hwanjeonhae juseyo.
dal-law/pa-oon-duh-ruhl won-hwa-ro hwan-jawn-eh joo-say-yo
dollar/pound won-into change please

How much is the commission?
수수료가 얼마예요? **susuryoga eolmayeyo?**
soo-soo-ryo-ga awl-ma-yay-yo
fee how-much-be

Could I just see your ID, please?
신분증 좀 보여 주세요. **sinbunjeung jom boyeo juseyo.**
shin-boon-jung jom po-yaw joo-say-yo
ID-card just present please

bank	은행 **eunhaeng**	*uhn-eng*
currency exchange	환전 **hwanjeon**	*hwan-jawn*
dollar	달러 **dalleo**	*tal-law*
dollar (Canadian ~)	캐나다 달러 **kaenada dalleo**	*keh-na-da tal-law*
euro	유로 **yuro**	*yoo-ro*
pound sterling	파운드 **paundeu**	*pa-oon-duh*
South African rand	남아프리카 랜드 **namapeurika raendeu**	*nam-a-puh-ree-ka ren-duh*
won	원 **won**	*won*

A US dollar, euro or British pound is worth over 1000 won, so you will feel rich when you change your money!

I would like the change in 10,000 won bills, please.
만원권 지폐로 주세요. **manwongwon jipyero juseyo.**
man-won-kwon chee-pay-ro choo-say-yo
10,000-won bill-in give

bill(s) / banknote(s)	지폐 **jipye**	*chee-pay*
coin(s)	동전 **dongjeon**	*tohng-jawn*
100 wons / 500 wons	백원 **baegwon** / 오백원 **obaegwon**	*peg-won / o-beg-won*
1000 wons / 5000 wons	천원 **cheonwon** / 오천원 **ocheonwon**	*chawn-won / o-chawn-won*
10,000 wons / 50,000 wons	만원 **manwon** / 오만원 **omanwon**	*man-won / o-man-won*

Flying

You're likely to arrive via Incheon International Airport.

We'll be taking off / landing in 30 minutes.
30분 후에 이륙하겠습니다 / 착륙하겠습니다.
samsip bun hue iryukagetseumnida/changnyukagetseumnida.
sam-ship poon oo-ay ee-rook-a-ge[t]-sum-nee-da / chang-nyook-a-ge[t]-sum-nee-da
30 minutes after-at take-off/land

Please board immediately at Gate 8.
8번 게이트로 즉시 탑승하시기 바랍니다.
pal beon geiteuro jeuksi tapseunghasigi baramnida.
pal bawn key-ee-tuh-ro ju[k]-shee tap-sung-ha-shi-gee pa-ram-nee-da
8 number gate-through immediately board please

airline company	항공사 **hanggongsa**	*hang-gong-sa*
airplane	비행기 **bihaenggi**	*pee-heng-gee*

baggage / carry-on baggage	위탁 수하물 **witak suhamul** / 기내 수하물 **ginae suhamul**	*wee-tak soo-a-mool / kee-nay soo-a-mool*
baggage (lost ~)	수하물 분실 **suhamul bunsil**	*soo-a-mool poon-shil*
boarding pass	탑승권 **tapseunggwon**	*tap-sung-gwon*
check-in	탑승 수속 **tapseung susok**	*tap-sung soo-sok*
flight (domestic ~)	국내선 **gungnaeseon**	*koong-neh-sawn*
flight (international ~)	국제선 **gukjeseon**	*kook-jay-sawn*
flight attendant	승무원 **seungmuwon**	*sung-moo-won*
in-flight meal	기내식 **ginaesik**	*kee-neh-sheek*
pilot	조종사 **jojongsa**	*cho-jong-sa*
seat number	좌석번호 **jwaseokbeonho**	*cha-sawk-pawn-ho*

What time are the flights to Jeju Island?
제주도행 비행기가 몇 시에 있어요?
jejudohaeng bihaenggiga myeot sie isseoyo?
chay-joo-doh-eng pee-heng-gee-ga myawt shee-ay eess-aw-yo
Jeju-Island-to flight what time-at there-is

What time does it depart/arrive?
몇 시에 출발해요 / 도착해요?
myeot sie chulbalhaeyo / dochakaeyo?
myawt shee-ay chool-bal-eh-yo / do-chak-eh-yo
what time-at depart/arrive

I would like an aisle seat, please.
복도쪽 좌석으로 주세요. **bokdojjok jwaseogeuro juseyo.**
pok-doh-CHOk chwa-sawg-uh-ro choo-say-yo
corridor-side seat-by give-please

window seat	창가 **changga**	*chang-ga*
at the front	앞쪽 **apjjok**	*ap-CHOk*

at the back	뒤쪽 **dwijjok**	*twee-CHO*ᵏ
in the middle	가운데 **gaunde**	*ka-oon-day*

Going by bus, train or boat

Bus

There are two types of long-distance express buses: standard and luxury. The only difference is the level of comfort. On long trips, buses stop about every two hours at rest areas, where you can buy snacks and regional specialities. Find out more at www.kobus.co.kr.

I'd like a one-way/single ticket, please.
편도 1 장 주세요. **pyeondo han jang juseyo.**
pyawn-do han jang joo-say-yo
one-way 1 unit give

express bus	고속버스 **gosokbeoseu**	*go-so*ᵏ*-paw-suh*
night bus	야간 **yagan/** 심야 **simya** 버스 **beoseu**	*ya-gan / sheem-ya paw-suh*
bus ticket	승차권 **seungchagwon**	*sung-cha-kwon*
round trip / return	왕복 **wangbok**	*wang-bo*ᵏ
reservation / booking	예약 **yeyak**	*yay-ya*ᵏ
advance purchase	예매 **yemae**	*yay-meh*
full fare	일반요금 **ilbanyogeum**	*eel-ban-yo-gum*
child fare	아동요금 **adongyogeum**	*a-dong-yo-gum*
discount	할인 **harin**	*har-een*
available seat	잔여 좌석 **janyeo jwaseok**	*chan-yaw cha-saw*ᵏ
sold out	매진 **maejin**	*meh-jeen*
exchange	교환 **gyohwan**	*kyo-hwan*
refund	환불 **hwanbul**	*han-bool*
timetable	시간표 **siganpyo**	*shee-gan-pyo*
regional speciality	특산물 **teuksanmul**	*tu*ᵏ*-san-mool*

Train

Korea has an excellent train network operated by KoRail. The fastest service is the high-speed KTX (Korea Train Express). The trains have cafés and various entertainment options – computer games and even karaoke. If you're a fan of K-drama, you might have noticed that train passengers eat hard-boiled eggs or sausages with soda. Take a picnic!

train journey	기차 여행 **gicha yeohaeng**	*kee-cha yaw-heng*
carriage 3, seat 11	3호차 11석 **sam hocha sibil seok**	*sam o-cha shib-il saw*[k]
standing room / seating	입석 **ipseok** / 좌석 **jwaseok**	*ip-saw*[k] */ cha-saw*[k]
ticket inspector	검표원 **geompyowon**	*kawm-pyo-won*
travelling without a ticket	무임승차 **muimseungcha**	*moo-eem-sung-cha*

Boat

You can get a ferry to Jeju Island, or to certain overseas destinations such as China, Russia or Japan.

ship	배 **bae**	*peh*
excursion boat	유람선 **yuramseon**	*yoo-ram-sawn*
sea	바다 **bada**	*pa-da*
lighthouse	등대 **deungdae**	*tung-deh*
port	항구 **hanggu**	*hang-goo*

Going by taxi

If the roof light of a taxi is on and indicates 빈 차 **bin cha** *empty car*, it's free and you can hail it.

There are two categories: 일반 택시 **ilban taeksi** *normal taxis* and 모범 택시 **mobeom taeksi** *luxury taxis*. The difference lies in the experience of the driver and the comfort of the vehicle.

Take me to the airport, please.
공항으로 가 주세요.
gonghangeuro ga juseyo.
kong-ang-uh-ro ka choo-say-yo
airport-to go please

Is it far from here?
여기에서 멀어요?
yeogieseo meoreoyo?
yaw-gee-ay-saw mawr-aw-yo
here-from be-far

Stop over there, please.
저쪽에 세워 주세요.
jeojjoge sewo juseyo.
chaw-cHog-ay say-wo choo-say-yo
over-there–at stop please

Can I pay by credit card?
카드로 계산돼요?
kadeuro gyesandwaeyo?
ka-duh-ro kay-san-teh-yo
card-by pay

taxi driver	택시 기사 **taeksi gisa**	*tek-shee gee-sa*
receipt	영수증 **yeongsujeung**	*yawng-soo-juhng*
additional charge	할증료 **haljeungnyo**	*hal-chung-nyo*
fare	요금 **yogeum**	*yo-gum*

In Korea, you can hire a sort of 'proxy driver' or chauffeur (대리 운전 **daeri unjeon**) to drive you to or from a location in your own car. It is a very convenient service that people often take advantage of if they go out drinking.

Could you please call a proxy driver for me?
대리 운전 좀 불러 주세요.
daeri unjeon jom bulleo juseyo.
teh-ree oon-jawn jom pool-law joo-say-yo
substitute driver just call please

Pick me up in front of City Hall, please.
시청 앞으로 와 주세요. **sicheong apeuro wa juseyo.**
shi-chawng ap-uh-ro wa choo-say-yo
city-hall front-to come please

Cycling

Korean cities are not well adapted for cycling. People ride bikes more for leisure than as a means of transport, so you're most likely to be able to rent them at certain tourist sites.

Do you have a child's bike?
어린이용 자전거 있어요? **eoriniyong jajeongeo isseoyo?**
aw-reen-ee-yong cha-jawn-gaw eess-aw-yo
child-for bicycle have

How much is a 1-hour rental?
한 시간에 얼마예요? **han sigane eolmayeyo?**
han shee-gan-ay awl-ma-ay-yo
one hour-per how-much-be

bicycle	자전거 **jajeongeo**	*cha-jawn-gaw*
tandem bicycle ('2 seater bicycle')	2 인승 자전거 **i inseung jajeongeo**	*ee in-sung cha-jawn-gaw*
bike rental	자전거 대여 **jajeongeo daeyeo**	*cha-jawn-gaw teh-yaw*
deposit	보증금 **bojeunggeum**	*po-jung-gum*
rental rate	대여 요금 **daeyeo yogeum**	*teh-yaw yo-gum*
additional charges	추가요금 **chugayogeum**	*choo-ga-yo-gum*

Motorcycles (오토바이 **otobai**) are used mainly for delivery services rather than for getting around.

Renting a car

To rent a car, you'll need an International Driving Permit and another form of identification.

I'd like to rent a car.
차를 빌리고 싶은데요. **chareul billigo sipeundeyo.**
cha-ruhl peel-lee-go ship-uhn-day-yo
car rent would-like-to

car rental	렌트카 **renteuka**	*ren-tuh-ka*
deposit	예약금 **yeyakgeum**	*yay-yak-gum*
rental conditions	대여 자격 **daeyeo jagyeok**	*teh-yaw cha-gaw^k*
pick-up date/time	대여 일시 **daeyeo ilsi**	*teh-yaw il-shee*
return date/time	반납 일시 **bannap ilsi**	*pan-na^p il-shee*
driver's licence	운전 면허증 **unjeon myeonheojeung**	*oon-jawn myawn-aw-chung*
International Driving Permit	국제 운전 면허증 **gukje unjeon myeonheojeung**	*goo^k-chay oon-jawn myawn-aw-chung*

Driving

Many petrol stations in Korea are still full service. An attendant will fill up your tank with the amount desired. Drivers are usually offered tissues and a bottle of mineral water or other services depending on the amount spent ... the extras are free!

Fill it up, please.
가득 채워 주세요.
gadeuk chaewo juseyo.
ka-duh^k cheh-o joo-say-yo
full fill-up please

Please put in 20 litres. (5 gallons)
20리터 넣어 주세요.
isim niteo neoeo juseyo.
ee-shim nee-taw naw-aw joo-say-yo
20 litre put-in please

car wash	세차장 **sechajang**	*say-cha-jang*
diesel	경유 **gyeongyu**	*kyawng-yoo*
petrol / gasoline	휘발유 **hwiballyu**	*hwee-bal-lyoo*
petrol/gas station	주유소 **juyuso**	*choo-yoo-so*

headlamps / headlights	전조등 **jeonjodeung /** 헤드라이트 **hedeuraiteu**	*chawn-jo-dung / hay-duh-ra-ee-tuh*
intersection	사거리 **sageori**	*sa-gaw-ree*
one-way street	일방통행 **ilbangtonghaeng**	*il-bahng-tong-heng*
parking	주차장 **juchajang**	*choo-cha-jang*
parking (no ~)	주차금지 **juchageumji**	*chu-cha-kum-jee*
pedestrian crossing	횡단보도 **hoengdanbodo**	*heng-dan-bo-do*
seat belt	안전벨트 **anjeonbelteu**	*an-jawn-pel-tuh*
traffic lights	신호등 **sinhodeung**	*shin-o-dung*
turn (left ~)	좌회전 **jwahoejeon**	*cha-hway-jawn*
turn (right ~)	우회전 **uhoejeon**	*oo-hway-jawn*

During the year-end holiday season, random stops to check the blood alcohol level of drivers are more frequent.

Could you please show me your driver's license?
면허증 좀 보여 주십시오.
myeonheojeung jom boyeo jusipsio.
myawn-haw-chung jom bo-yaw joo-ship-shee-o
driver's-license just present please

fine	과태료 **gwataeryo /** 벌금 **beolgeum**	*kwa-teh-ryo / pawl-gum*
sobriety test	음주단속 **eumjudansok**	*um-joo-dan-sok*
driving ban / suspended license	면허 정지 **myeonheo jeongji**	*myawn-haw chawng-jee*
blood alcohol level	혈중 알콜 농도 **hyeoljung alkol longdo**	*hyawl-choong al-kol long-doh*

On the road

Korean highways have rest areas that are more like shopping centres, with services such as ATMs, internet access, pharmacies and, of course, food and drinks!

How can I get onto the motorway/highway?
고속도로에 어떻게 가요?
gosokdoroe eotteoke gayo?
ko-sok-toh-ro-ay aw-ᴛaw-kay ka-yo
expressway-to how go

Where's the tollgate?
톨게이트가 어디예요?
tolgeiteuga eodiyeyo?
tol-gay-ee-tuh-ga aw-dee-yay-yo
tollgate where-be

I have a flat tire.
타이어가 펑크났어요.
taieoga peongkeunasseoyo.
ta-ee-aw-ga pawng-kuh-nass-aw-yo
tire is-punctured

entrance	입구 **ipgu**	*ip-goo*
exit	출구 **chulgu**	*chool-goo*
major road	국도 **gukdo**	*kook-toh*
rest area	휴게소 **hyugeso**	*hyoo-gay-so*
speed limit	제한 속도 **jehan sokdo**	*chay-han sok-toh*
traffic jam	교통 체증 **gyotong chejeung**	*kyo-tong chay-jung*

Getting around town

Finding your way around

Excuse me, could you tell me the way?
실례지만 길 좀 여쭤 볼게요.
sillyejiman gil jom yeojjwo bolgeyo?
shil-lay-jee-man keel jom yaw-CHO bol-gay-yo
impoliteness-but way please ask allow

How do I get to Insa-dong?
인사동에 어떻게 가요?
insadonge eotteoke gayo?
in-sa-dong-ay aw-TAW-kay ka-yo
Insa-dong-to how go

Is it far from here?
여기서 멀어요?
yeogiseo meoreoyo?
yaw-gee-saw mawr-aw-yo
here-from be-far

How long does it take to get to Insa-dong?
인사동까지 얼마나 걸려요?
insadongkkaji eolmana geollyeoyo?
in-sa-dong-KA-jee awl-ma-na kawl-law-yo
Insa-dong-to how-long take-time

Can I get there on foot / by bus / by metro?
걸어서 / 버스로 / 지하철로 갈 수 있어요?
georeoseo / beoseuro / jihacheollo gal su isseoyo?
kawr-aw-saw / paw-suh-ro / chee-a-chawl-lo kal soo eess-aw-yo
on-foot / by-bus / by-metro go can

The reply might be:

Go straight, to just over there.
저기까지 똑바로 가세요.
jeogikkaji ttokbaro gaseyo.
chaw-kee-KA-jee TOK-ba-ro ka-say-o
there-as-far-as straight go

Cross at the crosswalk.
횡단보도를 건너세요.
hoengdanbodoreul geonneoseyo.
heng-dan-bo-do-rul kawn-naw-say-o
crosswalk cross

Turn left.
왼쪽으로 도세요.
oenjjogeuro doseyo.
wen-CHOg-uh-ro to-say-yo
left-side-to turn

It is in front of the pedestrian flyover.
육교 앞에 있어요.
yukgyo ape isseoyo.
yook-gyo ap-ay eess-aw-yo
pedestrian-bridge front-in is-located

to the left / to the right	왼쪽 **oenjjok /** 오른쪽 **oreunjjok**	*wen-CHO^k / o-run-CHO^k*
in front / facing	앞 **ap**	*a^p*
at the back / behind	뒤 **dwi**	*twee*
at the side / next to	옆 **yeop**	*yaw^p*
street	길 **gil**	*keel*

Taking public transport

Four cities in Korea have metros–the most extensive is in Seoul. Its metro stations have shops where you can buy practically anything: from food and books to cosmetics and clothing. There are also free toilets at every station. Cities equally have efficient bus networks.

bus	버스 **beoseu**	*paw-suh*
bus stop	버스 정류장 **beoseu jeongnyujang**	*paw-suh chawng-nyoo-jang*
metro	지하철 **jihacheol**	*chee-a-chawl*
metro station	지하철역 **jihacheolyeok**	*chee-a-chawl-yaw^k*
toilet	화장실 **hwajangsil**	*hwa-jang-shil*
underground shopping centre	지하상가 **jihasangga**	*chee-ha-sang-ga*

To use public transit, you need a travel card, which you can buy in stations or certain shops. There is a rechargeable card or a single-use card. Remember to use it when entering and exiting a metro or bus. The card is automatically debited depending on the distance of your ride. If you don't validate it on exit, you'll have problems on your next entry.

travel card	교통 카드 **gyotong kadeu**	*ko-tong ka-duh*
amount	금액 **geumaek**	*kuhm-ay*[k]
recharge	충전 **chungjeon**	*choong-jawn*

If you need to ask another traveller for help:

Where is the nearest metro station?
가장 가까운 지하철역이 어디에 있어요?
gajang gakkaun jihacheollyeogi eodie isseoyo?
ka-jang ka-ка-oon chee-a-chawl-lyawk-ee aw-dee-ay eess-aw-yo
most be-near metro-station where-at is-located

Where do I get the number 100 bus?
100 번 버스를 어디에서 타요?
baek beon beoseureul eodieseo tayo?
pek bawn paw-suh-ruhl aw-dee-ay-saw ta-yo
100 number bus where-at take

Change at Myeong-dong.
명동에서 갈아타세요. **myeongdongeseo garataseyo.**
myawng-dong-ay-saw kar-a-ta-say-yo
Myeong-dong-at change

Get off at the next station.
다음 역에서 내리세요. **daeum yeogeseo naeriseyo.**
ta-uhm yawg-ay-saw neh-ree-say-yo
next station-at get-off

Take exit number 7.
7 번 출구로 나가세요. **chil beon chulguro nagaseyo.**
chil bawn chool-goo-ro na-ga-say-yo
7 number exit-through go-out

transfer / change	갈아타는 곳 **garataneun got**	*kar-a-ta-nun go^t*
metro map	지하철 노선도 **jihacheol noseondo**	*chee-a-chawl no-sawn-doh*
exit	나가는 곳 **naganeun got**	*na-ga-nun go^t*

Places of interest

South Korea has palaces, temples, art museums, history museums and war memorials to visit. Or if you want to experience local culture, try the vibrant traditional markets.

art	예술 **yesul**	*yay-sool*
crafts	공예 **gongye**	*kong-yay*
calligraphy	서예 **seoye**	*saw-yay*
sculpture	조각 **jogak**	*cho-ga^k*
museum	박물관 **bangmulgwan**	*pang-mool-gan*
pagoda	탑 **tap**	*tah^p*
Buddhist temple	절 **jeol**	*chawl*

Can I take a brochure?
안내책자를 가져도 될까요?
annaechaekjareul gajyeodo doelkkayo?
an-neh-chek-cha-ruhl ka-chaw-to dwel-ĸa-yo
brochure take can

Don't miss the 남대문 시장 **namdaemun sijang** *Namdaemun Market* in Seoul, the largest traditional market in Korea. Just about everything is sold here, and you can negotiate prices!

Could you give me a discount, please?
좀 깎아 주세요. **jom kkakka juseyo.**
chom ĸaĸ-a joo-say-yo
just lower-the-price please

Can you give me a bit more for the same price?
서비스로 더 주시면 안 돼요?
seobiseuro deo jusimyeon an dwaeyo?
saw-bee-suh-ro taw choo-shi-myawn an deh-yo
for-free more give-if not alright

Going to a performance

You can see performances of traditional Korean or classical Western forms of dance and music, not to mention contemporary genres such as K-pop. Korean films are increasingly popular worldwide. Foreign films are subtitled. The word for a ticket for a performance is 티켓 **tiket**.

What film is showing that you would recommend?
요즘 무슨 영화가 재미있어요?
yojeum museun yeonghwaga jaemiisseoyo?
yo-juhm moo-suhn yawng-wa-ga cheh-mee-eess-aw-yo
these-days what movie be-interesting

Is it subtitled in English?
영어 자막이 있어요? **yeongeo jamagi isseoyo?**
yawng-aw cha-mag-ee eess-aw-yo
English subtitle there-is

What time does the film start?
몇 시 영화예요? **myeot si yeonghwayeyo?**
myaw^t shee yawng-wa-yay-yo
what time film-be

cinema / movie theatre	영화관 **yeonghwagwan**	*yawng-wa-gwan*
foreign film	외국 영화 **oeguk yeonghwa**	*way-goo^k yawng-wa*
Korean film	한국 영화 **hanguk yeonghwa**	*han-goo^k yawng-wa*

To suggest going to see a performance, put the suffix 실래요 **-sillaeyo** after the verb stem of *to see* (or if the verb stem ends in a consonant, 으실래요 **-eusillaeyo**).

How about going to see a concert?
콘서트 보러 가실래요? **konseoteu boreo gasillaeyo?**
kon-saw-tuh po-raw ka-seel-leh-yo
concert see-in-order-to go

dance	춤 **chum** / 댄스 **daenseu**	*choom / dehn-s*
opera	오페라 **opera**	*o-pay-ra*
play / theatre	연극 **yeongeuk**	*yawn-guh^k*
show / performance	공연 **gongyeon**	*kong-yawn*

To ask someone's opinion, use 어떻다 **eotteota** *be how*.

How was the film?
영화가 어땠어요?
yeonghwaga eottaesseoyo?
yawng-wa-ga aw-tess-aw-yo
film be-how

It was touching.
감동적이었어요.
gamdongjeogieosseoyo.
kam-dong-jawg-ee-awss-aw-yo
touching-be

Posting a letter

To say how you want a letter to be sent, attach 으로 **-euro** *by (means of)* after the noun. (This becomes 로 **-ro** after a vowel.)

I'd like to send a postcard to Europe.
유럽에 엽서를 보내고 싶은데요.
yureobe yeopseoreul bonaego sipeundeyo.
yoo-rawb-ay yawp-saw-ruhl po-neh-go ship-uhn-day-yo
Europe-to postcard send would-like-to

I'd like to send a postcard to North America / South Africa / New Zealand / Britain / Australia.
북아메리카 / 남아프리카 / 뉴질랜드 / 영국 / 호주에 엽서를 보내고 싶은데요.
bugamerika / namapeurika / nyujillaendeu / yeongguk / hojue yeopseoreul bonaego sipeundeyo.
poog-ah-may-ree-kah / nam-a-puh-ree-ka / nyoo-jeel-len-duh / yawng-goo[k] / ho-joo-ay yawp-saw-ruhl po-neh-go ship-uhn-day-yo
North America / South Africa / New Zealand / Britain / Australia-to postcard send would-like-to

I'd like to send this by express mail.
빠른우편으로 보내 주세요.
ppareunupyeoneuro bonae juseyo.
Pa-ruhn-uh-pyawn-uh-ro po-neh joo-say-yo
fast-mailing-by send please

Five stamps, please.
우표 5 장 주세요.
upyo daseot jang juseyo.
oo-pyo ta-saw[t] jang joo-say-yo
stamp 5 unit please

post office	우체국 **ucheguk**	*oo-chay-goo*[k]
postbox / mailbox	우체통 **uchetong**	*oo-chay-tong*
by air	항공편으로 **hanggongpyeoneuro**	*hang-gong-pyawn-uh-ro*
by ship	배편으로 **baepyeoneuro**	*peh-pyawn-uh-ro*
express mail service	**EMS**	*ee-em-es*
parcel / package	소포 **sopo**	*so-po*
parcel service	택배 **taekbae**	*tek-beh*
regular mail / surface mail	보통 우편 **botong upyeon**	*bo-tong oo-pyawn*

Making a phone call

Rather than saying 'Goodbye' before hanging up, Koreans either say an elongated 네 **ne** *Yes* (casual) or 들어가세요 **deureogaseyo** (polite) *Go right in*. The honorific 씨 **ssi** *[shee]* is used after someone's given name if you know them well, or after both names (surname + given name) if you don't.

Hello?
여보세요. **yeoboseyo.**
yaw-bo-say-yo

Is Yumi there?
유미 씨 있어요? **yumi ssi isseoyo?**
yoo-mee shee eess-aw-yo

Is this the residence of Ms Yumi Kim?
김유미 씨 댁인가요? **gimyumi ssi daegingayo?**
keem-yoo-mee shee tehk-een-ga-yo
Kim-Yu-Mi Ms residence-be

I'd like to speak to Yumi, please.
실례지만, 유미 씨 좀 바꿔 주세요.
sillyejiman, yumi ssi jom bakkwo juseyo.
shil-lay-jee-man yoo-mee shee jom ba-kwo joo-say-yo
impoliteness-but, Yumi Ms just pass please

Could I have a contact number for Jerome?
제롬 씨 연락처 좀 알 수 있을까요?
jerom ssi yeollakcheo jom al su isseulkkayo?
chay-rom shee yawl-lak-chaw jom al soo eess-uhl-κa-yo
Jerome Mr contact-number just know can

Goodbye. (polite)
아, 예. 들어가세요. **a, ye. deureogaseyo.**
ah yay. tuhr-aw-ga-say-yo

Bye. (casual)
네. **ne.**
naaay (elongated)

phone	전화 **jeonhwa**	*chawn-ha*
phone number	전화번호 **jeonhwabeonho**	*chawn-ah-bawn-o*
text message / SMS	문자메시지 **munjamesiji**	*moon-ja-may-shee-jee*

I'd like to buy a SIM card. ('SIM-card buy I'd-like')
심카드를 사려고 하는데요.
simkadeureul saryeogo haneundeyo.
shim-ka-duh-ruhl sa-raw-go ha-nuhn-day-yo

Could you show me your ID, please? ('ID-card present please')
신분증을 보여 주세요.
sinbunjeungeul boyeo juseyo.
shin-boon-chung-uhl po-yaw joo-say-yo

Going online

In Korea, wi-fi is everywhere and the connection is very fast.

Is there wi-fi here?
무선 인터넷이 되나요?
museon inteonesi doenayo?
moo-sawn een-taw-naysh-ee tway-na-yo
wireless internet be-possible

What's the password?
비밀 번호가 뭐예요?
bimil beonhoga mwoyeyo?
pee-mil bawn-o-ga mwo-yay-yo
secret number what-be

computer	컴퓨터 **keompyuteo**	*kawm-pyoo-taw*
connection	접속 **jeopsok**	*chawp-so^{k}*
download	다운로드 **daunnodeu**	*ta-oon-no-duh*
email	이메일 **imeil**	*ee-may-il*
ID	아이디 **aidi**	*a-ee-dee*
internet	인터넷 **inteonet**	*in-taw-nay^{t}*
internet café	**PC**방 **bang**	*PC bahng*
keyboard	키보드 **kibodeu**	*kee-bo-duh*
mouse	마우스 **mauseu**	*ma-oo-suh*
screen	모니터 **moniteo**	*mo-nee-taw*
site	싸이트 **ssaiteu /** 누리집 **nurijip**	*sa-ee-tuh /* *noo-ree-jee^{p}*
USB flash drive	**USB** 메모리 **memori**	*USB may-mo-ree*
wireless internet / *wi-fi*	무선 인터넷 **museon inteonet /** 와이파이 **waipai**	*moo-sawn in-taw-nay^{t} /* *wa-ee-pa-ee*

Official business

The names of official documents often end with the term 증 **jeung** *certificate, card*.

alien registration card	외국인 등록증 **oegugin deungnokjeung**	*way-goog-een* *tung-no^{k}-chung*
consulate	영사관 **yeongsagwan**	*yawng-sa-gwan*
embassy	대사관 **daesagwan**	*teh-sa-gwan*
ID card	신분증 **sinbunjeung**	*sheen-boon-jung*
passport	여권 **yeogwon**	*yaw-kwon*
stay	체류 **cheryu**	*chay-ryoo*
visa	비자 **bija**	*pee-ja*

At the bank

Two common banking actions are 돈을 찾다 **doneul chatda** *to withdraw money* and 돈을 부치다 **doneul buchida** *to send money*. Note the common word 돈 **don** *money*!

I'd like to withdraw some money / open a bank account.
돈을 찾고 / 은행 계좌를 열고 싶은데요.
doneul chatgo / eunhaeng gyejwareul yeolgo sipeundeyo.
tohn-uhl chat-go / un-eng gay-jwa-ruhl yawl-go ship-uhn-day-yo
money withdraw / bank account open would-like-to

How do I use the ATM / cash dispenser?
현금 인출기를 어떻게 사용하나요?
hyeongeum inchulgireul eotteoke sayonghanayo?
hyawn-guhm een-shool-gee-ruhl aw-ᴛaw-kay sa-yong-ha-na-yo
cash teller-machine how use

bank	은행 **eunhaeng**	*un-eng*
cash	현금 **hyeongeum**	*hyawn-guhm*
cash dispenser / ATM	현금 인출기 **hyeongeum inchulgi / ATM**	*hyawn-guhm een-chool-kee / ATM*
currency exchange	환전 **hwanjeon**	*hwan-jawn*
deposit	입금 **ipgeum**	*eep-guhm*
withdrawal	출금 **chulgeum**	*chool-guhm*

At the hairdresser's

A Korean hairdresser's is almost like a tea room. People go without an appointment and are served tea or other drinks and are sometimes even given a manicure kit to pass the time while waiting their turn!

How would you like your hair done?
어떻게 해 드릴까요?
eotteoke hae deurilkkayo?
aw-ᴛaw-kay heh tuh-reel-ᴋa-yo
how do would-you-like

Like this!
이렇게요.
ireokeyo.
ee-raw-kay-yo
in-this-way

I'd like this hairstyle.
이 스타일로 해 주세요. **i seutaillo hae juseyo.**
ee suh-ta-eel-lo heh joo-say-yo
this style-as do please

I'd like a haircut.
커트해 주세요. **keoteuhae juseyo.**
kaw-tuh-eh joo-say-yo
cut please

hair	머리 **meori /** 머리카락 **meorikarak**	*maw-ree / maw-ree-ka-ra*^{k}
hair (curly ~)	곱슬머리 **gopseulmeori**	*ko*^{p}*-suhl-maw-ree*
hair (straight ~)	생머리 **saengmeori**	*seng-maw-ree*
hair (long / short ~)	긴 **gin /** 짧은 **jjalbeun** 머리 **meori**	*geen maw-ree / ᴄʜal-bun maw-ree*
hairdresser	미용사 **miyongsa /** 헤어 디자이너 **heeo dijaineo**	*mee-yong-sa / hay-aw dee-ja-ee-naw*
hair salon	미용실 **miyongsil /** 헤어숍 **heeosyop**	*mee-yong-shil / hay-aw-shyop*
blow-dry	드라이 **deurai**	*tuh-ra-ee*
bobbed	단발머리 **danbalmeori**	*tan-bal-maw-ree*
colouring / dye	염색 **yeomsaek**	*yawm-seh*^{k}
dark / light colour	어두운 **eoduun /** 밝은 **balgeun** 색 **saek**	*aw-doo-oon se*^{k} */ pal-guhn se*^{k}
permanent wave	웨이브 파마 **weibeu pama**	*wayee-buh pa-ma*
straightened	매직 **maejik**	*meh-jee*^{k}

↗ Outdoors

Recreational sports

At the weekend, many Koreans enjoy 등산 **deungsan** *hiking, mountaineering, climbing*. To say you practice a sport, 하다 **hada** *to do* is used for most activities, but 치다 **chida** *to hit* is used for sports using a racket or bat (apart from baseball, which takes **hada**), and 타다 **tada** *to ride* is used for sports that involve riding something – including with your feet (e.g. skiing, skating, etc.)!

씨름 **ssireum** is a traditional national sport that is somewhat similar to sumo wrestling.

Shall we ...		
do taekwondo?	태권도 하러 **taegwondo hareo**	*teh-kwon-doh ha-raw*
go skiing?	스키 타러 **seuki tareo**	*suh-kee ta-raw*
play tennis?	테니스 치러 **teniseu chireo**	*tay-nee-s chee-raw*
	...갈까요? **galkkayo?**	*kal-ка-yo*

sport	스포츠 **seupocheu** / 운동 **undong**	*s-po-chuh* / *oon-dong*

badminton	배드민턴 **baedeuminteon**	*peh-duh-min-tawn*
baseball	야구 **yagu**	*ya-goo*
basketball	농구 **nonggu**	*nong-goo*
football / soccer	축구 **chukgu**	*chook-goo*
hapkido (martial art)	합기도 **hapgido**	*hap-gee-do*
jogging	조깅 **joging**	*jo-ging*
skating (ice ~)	스케이트 **seukeiteu**	*s-kay-ee-tuh*
skating (roller ~)	롤러 스케이트 **rolleo seukeiteu**	*rol-law s-kay-ee-tuh*
ssireum (wrestling)	씨름 **ssireum**	*shee-ruhm*

At the pool or beach

In public pools, you are required to wear a 수영모 **suyeongmo** *swimming cap* and 수경 **sugyeong** *swimming goggles*. The word for *swimming* is 수영 **suyeong**. During the summer, the beaches get very crowded. The most famous beaches are around Busan.

Is the water deep / shallow?
수심이 깊어요 / 얕아요? **susimi gipeoyo / yatayo?**
soo-sheem-ee keep-aw-yo / yat-a-yo
depth-water be-deep / be-shallow

beach	해수욕장 **haesuyokjang**	*heh-soo-yok-jang*
changing room	탈의실 **taruisil**	*tar-ee-shil*
diving	다이빙 **daibing**	*ta-ee-ping*
life jacket	구명조끼 **gumyeongjokki**	*koo-myawng-jo-ĸee*
No swimming	수영 금지 **suyeong geumji**	*soo-yawng kuhm-jee*
river	강 **gang**	*kahng*
sea / ocean	바다 **bada**	*pa-da*
shower stall	샤워실 **syawosil**	*sha-wo-shil*
sunglasses	선글라스 **seongeullaseu**	*sawn-guhl-la-s*
swim ring (inner tube)	튜브 **tyubeu**	*tyoo-buh*
swimsuit	수영복 **suyeongbok**	*soo-yawng-bo^k*

Camping

Tent camping is becoming increasingly popular in Korea. You can also rent a camper. Often botanical gardens are located near campsites, so you can make the most of nature!

Where is the nearest campsite?
가까운 캠핑장이 어디에 있어요?
gakkaun kaempingjangi eodie isseoyo?
ka-ka-oon kem-ping-jang-ee aw-dee-ay eess-aw-yo
near campsite where-at be-located

2 days / 1 night	1박 2일 **il bak i il**	*il bak ee il*
off-season	비수기 **bisugi**	*pee-soo-kee*
peak season	성수기 **seongsugi**	*sawng-soo-kee*

camping stove ('gas burner')	가스 버너 **gaseu beoneo**	*ka-suh paw-naw*
flashlight / torch	손전등 **sonjeondeung**	*son-chawn-dung*
hammer / mallet	망치 **mangchi**	*mang-chee*
ice chest / cooler	아이스박스 **aiseubakseu**	*a-ee-s-bak-suh*
inflatable mattress	튜브 매트리스 **tyubeu maeteuriseu**	*tyoo-buh meh-tuh-ree-suh*
lighter	라이터 **raiteo**	*ra-ee-taw*
mosquito net	모기장 **mogijang**	*mo-kee-jang*
sleeping bag	침낭 **chimnang**	*chim-nang*
tent	텐트 **tenteu**	*ten-tuh*
tent pegs	텐트 말뚝 **tenteu malttuk**	*ten-tuh mal-TOOk*

Plants and animals

Plants

The traditional Korean painting known as 사군자 **sagunja** ('The Four Virtuous Plants') features four flowering plants that represent the seasons: 매화 **maehwa** *plum* (spring), 난초 **nancho** *orchid* (summer), 국화 **gukwa** *chrysanthemum* (autumn) and 대나무 **daenamu** *bamboo* (winter).

In the countryside you will also see 개나리 **gaenari** *forsythia* and 진달래 **jindallae** *azaleas* blooming in the spring, 나팔꽃 **napalkkot** *morning glory* and 장미 **jangmi** *wild roses* in the summer, 코스모스 **koseumoseu** *cosmos* in the autumn and 동백 **dongbaek** *camellias* in the winter.

What is the name of this flower?
이 꽃 이름이 뭐예요?
i kkot ireumi mwoyeyo?
ee ko[t] ee-ruhm-ee mwo-yay-yo
this flower name what-be

It's really beautiful!
정말 아름다워요.
jeongmal areumdawoyo.
chawng-mal a-ruhm-da-wo-yo
really be-beautiful

flower	꽃 **kkot**	*ko[t]*
plant	식물 **singmul**	*shing-mool*
tree	나무 **namu**	*na-moo*

Mammals

According to the foundation myth of the country (단군신화 **dangunsinhwa** *the Legend of Dangun*), the ancestors of Koreans are bears, making these valued animals in Korea. The verb 키우다 **kiuda** *to keep, to rear, to raise* is used to refer to having pets.

Do you have a pet?
애완동물 키우세요? **aewandongmul kiuseyo?**
eh-wan-dong-mool kee-oo-say-yo
pet-animal raise

animal	동물 **dongmul**	*tong-mool*
bear	곰 **gom**	*kom*
cat	고양이 **goyangi**	*ko-yang-ee*
cow / ox	소 **so**	*so*
dog	개 **gae**	*keh*

horse	말 **mal**	*mal*
monkey	원숭이 **wonsungi**	*won-soong-ee*
pig	돼지 **dwaeji**	*tweh-jee*
sheep	양 **yang**	*yang*
tiger	호랑이 **horangi**	*ho-rang-ee*

Birds

In Korea, the crow is seen as an ominous portent, while the magpie is considered a bird of good omen. According to a proverb, 'The song of the magpie invites welcome visitors.'

bird	새 **sae**	*seh*
chick	병아리 **byeongari**	*pyawng-a-ree*
chicken	닭 **dak**	*ta*^{k}
crow	까마귀 **kkamagwi**	*ᴋa-ma-gwee*
duck	오리 **ori**	*o-ree*
eagle	독수리 **doksuri**	*tok-soo-ree*
magpie	까치 **kkachi**	*ᴋa-chee*
nest	둥지 **dungji**	*toong-jee*
pigeon	비둘기 **bidulgi**	*pee-dool-kee*
sparrow	참새 **chamsae**	*cham-seh*

Fish and shellfish

There are two terms for *fish*: 물고기 **mulgogi** is the animal and 생선 **saengseon** is the food. A dish that divides opinion is 산낙지 **sannakji**, which is live octopus, sliced into small, squirming pieces. It must be chewed very thoroughly.

cod	대구 **daegu**	*teh-goo*
eel	장어 **jangeo**	*chang-aw*
hairtail / cutlassfish	갈치 **galchi**	*kal-chee*
loach / mudfish	미꾸라지 **mikkuraji**	*mee-ᴋoo-ra-jee*

lobster	바닷가재 **badatgajae**	*pa-da^t-ka-jeh*
mackerel	고등어 **godeungeo**	*ko-duhng-aw*
mussels	홍합 **honghap**	*hong-a^p*
octopus	낙지 **nakji**	*nak-chee*
oysters	굴 **gul**	*kool*
raw fish	회 **hoe**	*hay*
salmon	연어 **yeoneo**	*yawn-aw*
shellfish	조개 **jogae**	*cho-geh*
shrimp / prawns	새우 **saeu**	*seh-oo*
squid	오징어 **ojingeo**	*o-jing-aw*
tuna	참치 **chamchi**	*cham-chee*

Insects

Outdoors, summer brings 매미 **maemi** *cicadas* as well as 모기 **mogi** *mosquitoes* and 파리 **pari** *flies*, while autumn ushers in 귀뚜라미 **gwitturami** *crickets* and 잠자리 **jamjari** *dragonflies*. Some insects are eaten – you might see street vendors selling steamed or boiled 번데기 **beondegi** *silkworm pupae*. They may not look very appetizing, but are rich in protein and low in cholesterol, and are seasoned for taste.

I'm afraid of hornets.
말벌이 무서워요.
malbeori museowoyo.
mal-bawr-ee moo-saw-wo-yo
hornet be-scary

I hate spiders.
거미를 싫어해요.
geomireul sireohaeyo.
kaw-mee-ruhl shir-aw-heh-yo
spider hate

insect	곤충 **gonchung**	*kon-choong*
ant	개미 **gaemi**	*keh-mee*
bee	벌 **beol**	*pawl*
butterfly	나비 **nabi**	*na-bee*

earthworm	지렁이 **jireongi**	*chee-rawng-ee*

insecticide	살충제 **salchungje**	*sal-choong-jay*
mosquito repellent	모기약 **mogiyak**	*mo-kee-ya*[k]

Accommodation

There is a large choice of accommodation types, from modest low-price hotels (여관 **yeogwan**) to B&B-type guestrooms (민박 **minbak**) to traditional Korean guesthouses (한옥 민박 **hanok minbak**). In the countryside and quiet towns, you can stay in a 펜션 **pensyeon**, lodging with a private bathroom and kitchen.

guesthouse (can be a guestroom or hostel)	게스트 하우스 **geseuteu hauseu**	*gay-suh-tuh ha-oo-suh*
guestroom / B&B	민박 **minbak**	*meen-ba*[k]
holiday rooms/cabin	펜션 **pensyeon**	*pen-shawn*
hotel	호텔 **hotel**	*ho-tel*
hotel (low-price ~)	여관 **yeogwan**	*yaw-gwan*
motel	모텔 **motel**	*mo-tel*
single room	1인실 **il insil /** 싱글룸 **singgeullum**	*eel een-shil / shing-gul-lum*
double room	2인실 **i insil /** 더블룸 **deobeullum**	*ee een-shil / taw-buhl-loom*
family room	가족실 **gajoksil**	*ka-jok-shil*

Making a reservation

When booking a room, specify the dates with 부터 **buteo** *from* and 까지 **kkaji** *until*. The month comes before the day.

I'd like to make a reservation.
예약을 하고 싶은데요. **yeyageul hago sipeundeyo.**
yay-yag-uhl ha-go ship-uhn-day-yo
reservation do would-like-to

From 1 to 15 August, please.
8월 1일부터 15일까지요.
palwol il ilbuteo sibo ilkkajiyo.
par-ol eel il-boo-taw shi-bo il-ка-jee-yo
8-month 1 day-from 15 day-to

We will arrive at 4 p.m.
오후 4시에 도착해요.
ohu ne sie dochakaeyo.
o-hoo nay shi-ay to-chak-eh-yo
afternoon 4 hour-at arrive

Is it possible to change the reservation?
예약 변경 가능해요? **yeyak byeongyeong ganeunghaeyo?**
yay-ya[k] pyawn-gawng ka-nung-eh-yo
reservation modification be-possible

cancellation	취소 **chwiso**	*chee-so*
cancellation fee	취소 수수료 **chwiso susuryo**	*chee-so soo-soo-ryo*

At the hotel

On arrival, specify if you have already reserved a room:
예약했어요 **yeyakaesseoyo** *I have reserved.*
예약 안 했어요 **yeyak an haesseoyo** *I have not reserved.*

reception/information desk	리셉션 **risepsyeon** / 안내 **annae**	*ree-sep-shawn / an-neh*

I have a reservation in the name of Yumi Kim.
김유미로 예약했는데요. **gimyumiro yeyakaenneundeyo.**
kim-yoo-mee-ro yay-yak-en-nuhn-day-yo
Kim-Yu-Mi-by reserve

Can you complete this document?
이 서류를 작성해 주시겠어요?
i seoryureul jakseonghae jusigesseoyo?
ee saw-ryoo-ruhl chak-sawng-eh joo-shi-gayss-aw-yo
this document complete please

What time do we need to check out?
퇴실시간이 언제예요? **toesilsigani eonjeyeyo?**
tay-shil-shee-gan-ee awn-jay-yay-yo
checkout-time when-be

We would like breakfast included.
조식 포함해 주세요. **josik pohamhae juseyo.**
cho-shee[k] po-ham-eh joo-say-yo
breakfast include please

We don't want breakfast. ('breakfast not do')
조식은 안 할게요. **josigeun an halgeyo.**
cho-sheeg-uhn an al-kay-yo

check in	체크인 **chekeuin /** 입실 **ipsil**	*che-kuh-in / eep-shil*
check out	체크아웃 **chekeuaut /** 퇴실 **toesil**	*chay-kuh-a-oot / tway-shil*

Services and breakfast

To request a service, add the following suffix to the verb stem: ㄹ **-l** (after a vowel) / 을 **-eul** (after a consonant) + 수 있어요? **su isseoyo** *Can I ...?* e.g. 인터넷 하다 **inteonet hada** *to connect to the internet* → 인터넷 할 수 있어요? **inteonet hal su isseoyo?** *Can I connect to the internet?*

Could you call a taxi, please?
택시 좀 불러 주시겠어요? **taeksi jom bulleo jusigesseoyo?**
tek-shee jom pool-law joo-shee-gayss-aw-yo
taxi just call please

Is it possible to change the sheets? ('sheet change can?')
시트 갈 수 있어요? **siteu gal su isseoyo?**
shee-tuh kal soo eess-aw-yo

Can I ...		
have a city map?	도시 지도를 얻을 **dosi jidoreul eodeul**	*to-shee chi-do-ruhl awd-uhl*
change rooms?	방을 바꿀 **bangeul bakkul**	*pang-uhl pa-KOOl*
leave my luggage with you?	짐을 맡길 **jimeul matgil**	*chim-uhl mat-kil*
	...수 있어요? **su isseoyo?**	*soo eess-aw-yo*

Is there room service?

룸 서비스 가능해요? **rum seobiseu ganeunghaeyo?**

room saw-bee-suh ka-nuhng-heh-yo

room service be-possible

Breakfast

A traditional Korean breakfast consists of similar foods as at lunch or dinner, although today in a hotel 뷔페 **bwipe** *buffet* you will also often find Western breakfast foods. If you want to try 한식 **hansik** *Korean food* at breakfast, some standard options are rice, soup, meat or fish and a variety of vegetable side dishes, including sprouts, tofu and the ubiquitous 김치 **gimchi** *kimchi* (spicy pickled vegetables – usually cabbage).

breakfast	조식 **josik /** 아침식사 **achimsiksa**	*cho-shi*[k] */ a-chim-shi*[k]*-sa*
bread	빵 **ppang**	*Pang*
butter	버터 **beoteo**	*paw-taw*
cereal	씨리얼 **ssirieol**	*shee-ree-awl*
coffee	커피 **keopi**	*kaw-pee*
fruit juice	주스 **juseu**	*joo-suh*
hot chocolate	핫초코 **hatchoko**	*ha*[t]*-cho-ko*
jam	잼 **jaem**	*jem*

milk	우유 **uyu**	*oo-yoo*
sugar	설탕 **seoltang**	*sawl-tang*
tea	차 **cha**	*cha*

Resolving issues

If something doesn't work properly, the negation marker 안 **an** *not* is put before the verb.

The lamp doesn't work.
불이 안 들어와요.
buri an deureowayo.
poor-ee an tuhr-aw-wa-yo
lamp not light

There's no hot water.
따뜻한 물이 안 나와요.
ttatteutan muri an nawayo.
ᴛa-ᴛuht-an moor-ee an na-wa-yo
warm water not flow

I can't access the internet. ('internet not work')
인터넷이 안 되는데요. **inteonesi an doeneundeyo.**
in-taw-naysh-ee an day-nuhn-day-yo

If you need something, after the item add ...얻을 수 있어요? **...eodeul su isseoyo?** *Can I get a/some ...?*

toiletries	세면도구 **semyeondogu**	*say-myawn-doh-goo*
disposable ...	일회용 **ilhoeyong**	*il-way-yong*
... comb	빗 **bit**	*pee^{t}*
... razor	면도기 **myeondogi**	*myawn-doh-kee*
... toothbrush	칫솔 **chitsol**	*chi^{t}-sol*
sanitary towel	생리대 **saengnidae**	*seng-nee-deh*
shampoo	샴푸 **syampu**	*sham-poo*
soap	비누 **binu**	*pee-noo*
toilet paper / paper hankies	화장지 **hwajangji /** 휴지 **hyuji**	*hwa-jang-jee / hyoo-jee*
toothpaste	치약 **chiyak**	*chee-ya^{k}*

Checking out

Here are some terms for asking a price: 금액 **geumaek** *amount*, 요금 **yogeum** *charge, fee, rate*, 비용 **biyong** *cost, expense.*

How would you like to pay?
결제는 어떻게 하시겠어요?
gyeoljeneun eotteoke hasigesseoyo?
kawl-chay-nun aw-ттaw-kay ha-shee-gayss-aw-o
payment how do

By Visa card, please.
비자 카드로 해 주세요.
bija kadeuro hae juseyo.
pee-ja ka-duh-ro heh joo-say-o
Visa card-by do please

balance	잔금 **jangeum**	*chan-guhm*
bill / receipt	영수증 **yeongsujeung**	*yawng-soo-jung*
cash (in ~)	현금으로 **hyeongeumeuro**	*hawn-guh-muh-ro*
deposit	예약금 **yeyakgeum**	*yay-yak-guhm*
sales tax	부가세 **bugase**	*poo-ga-say*
surcharge	추가요금 **chugayogeum**	*choo-ga-yo-guhm*

Eating and drinking

Generally, Koreans eat lunch around noon and dinner around 6 p.m. But most restaurants are open non-stop until 11 p.m., and some are even open 24 hours a day. There is also a diverse choice of street food (길거리 음식 **gilgeori eumsik**). Korean food (한식 **hansik**) is healthy and delicious, with meals centred around rice, soup and a wide variety of side dishes. But you can also find restaurants offering other types of cuisine.

What kind of food do you like? ('what food like')
무슨 음식 좋아해요? **museun eumsik joahaeyo?**
moo-suhn um-shi[k] cho-a-eh-yo

Korean fast food	분식집 **bunsikjip**	*poon-shi[k]-chee[p]*
Korean restaurant	한식집 **hansikjip /** 한식당 **hansikdang**	*han-shi[k]- chee[p] / han-shi[k]-tang*
Korean table d'hote (full-course set meal)	한정식 **hanjeongsik**	*han-jawng-shi[k]*
Korean traditional food	전통 음식 **jeontong eumsik**	*chawn-tong uhm-shi[k]*
Chinese food	중국 음식 **jungguk eumsik /** 중국 요리 **jungguk yori**	*choong-goo[k] um-shi[k] / joong-goo[k] yo-ree*
Chinese restaurant	중국집 **junggukjip /** 중식당 **jungsikdang**	*choong-goo[k]-chee[p] / choong-shi[k]-tang*
French restaurant	프랑스 레스토랑 **peurangseu reseutorang**	*puh-rang-suh ray-suh-to-rang*
Japanese food	일본 음식 **ilbon eumsik /** 일본 요리 **ilbon yori**	*eel-bon um-shi[k] / eel-bon yo-ree*
Japanese restaurant	일식당 **ilsikdang /** 일식집 **ilsikjip**	*eel-shi[k]-tang / eel-shi[k]-chee[p]*
Western food restaurant	양식집 **yangsikjip /** 양식당 **yangsikdang**	*yang-shi[k]-chee[p] / yang-shi[k]-tang*
upmarket restaurant	고급 식당 **gogeup sikdang**	*ko-gup shi[k]-tang*
cheap restaurant	저렴한 식당 **jeoryeomhan sikdang**	*chaw-rawm-han shi[k]-tang*

At the restaurant

Usually you can sit where you want in a restaurant. A reservation is only needed at the finest establishments. In some places, you might need to specify whether you want to sit at a 테이블 **teibeul** *table* or in the 방 **bang** *room*. In the latter, you sit on a cushion on the floor and will need to take off your shoes.

Welcome!
어서 오세요. **eoseo oseyo.**
aw-saw o-say-yo
quick come

How many are you?
몇 분이세요? **myeot buniseyo?**
myaw[t] poon-ee-say-yo
how-many person-be

A place at a table, please.
테이블로 주세요. **teibeullo juseyo.**
tay-ee-bul-lo joo-say-yo
table-in please

A place in the room, please.
방으로 주세요. **bangeuro juseyo.**
pang-uh-ro joo-say-yo
room-in please

reservation	예약석 **yeyakseok**	*yay-yak-saw[k]*
waiter / waitress / restaurant employee	식당 종업원 **sikdang jongeobwon**	*shik-dang chong-aw-bwon*

A typical Korean meal doesn't have courses – dishes are served with various accompaniments all at once. The food can be spicy, often containing 고추장 **gochujang**, a fermented red chili paste.

Not too spicy, please.
안 맵게 해 주세요.
an maepge hae juseyo.
an mep-gay heh joo-say-yo
not be-spicy do give-please

The same thing, please.
같은 걸로 주세요.
gateun geollo juseyo.
kat-uhn gawl-lo joo-say-yo
same thing-as give-please

I'm a vegetarian.
채식주의예요.
chaesikjuuiyeyo.
cheh-shik-choo-ee-yay-yo
vegetarian-be

I'm allergic to fish.
생선 알레르기가 있어요.
saengseon allereugiga isseoyo.
seng-sawn al-lay-ruh-gee-ga eess-aw-yo
fish allergy there-is

Is there pork in this dish?
돼지고기가 들어가요? **dwaejigogiga deureogayo?**
tweh-jee-go-gee-ga tuhr-aw-ga-yo
pork be-included

The cutlery provided is a 숟가락 **sutgarak** *spoon* along with metal 젓가락 **jeotgarak** *chopsticks*. If you need one, you can ask for a 포크 **pokeu** *fork*. When you are finished, you can request the bill: 계산서 좀 주세요. **gyesanseo jom juseyo**. *The bill, please.* Typically, people don't tip at restaurants.

Excuse me, can we take the rest home?
이모! 남은 거 싸 주세요. **imo! nameun geo ssa juseyo?**
ee-mo! nam-uhn gaw ssa joo-say-yo
aunt remaining thing pack please
(customer addressing a waitress of a certain age)

Specialities and traditional dishes

A Korean meal typically consists of a bowl of rice, a soup or stew and a number of 반찬 **banchan** *[pan-chan] side dishes*, including 김치 **gimchi** *kimchi*. This national dish is made from spicy fermented vegetables – typically Chinese cabbage, white radish or cucumber, but there are many varieties. It is also used as a main ingredient in certain dishes.

There are several types of soups and stews:

- 국 **guk** *[kook]* and 탕 **tang** *[tang]* are soups with meat (pork, beef or chicken), fish or vegetables.
- 찌개 **jjigae** *[cHee-geh]* and 전골 **jeongol** *[chawn-gol]* are thicker stews or casseroles with less broth. They tend to be more salty and spicy.

Some other popular dishes are:

- 김밥 **gimbap** *[keem-ba^p]* (김 *seaweed* + 밥 *rice*) is rice and any combination of vegetables, meat, tofu or eggs rolled in a sheet of dried seaweed and cut into slices.
- 전 **jeon** *[chawn]* is a Korean-style pancake made with meat, poultry, seafood or vegetables, coated with batter and then panfried.
- 불고기 **bulgogi** *[pool-go-kee]* (불 *fire* + 고기 *meat*) is grilled beef (usually thinly sliced sirloin) marinated in soy sauce.
- 비빔밥 **bibimbap** *[pee-bim-pa^p]* (비빔 *mixing* + 밥 *rice*) is a bowl of rice topped with vegetables, meat and red chili paste, which is all mixed together after serving.
- 삼겹살 **samgyeopsal** *[sam-gyawp-sal]* *grilled pork belly*. This dish, as well as 불고기 **bulgogi**, is eaten with rice in bite-sized pieces wrapped in a lettuce leaf. It's common to share when eating out with family, friends or colleagues.
- 미역국 **miyeokguk** *[mee-yawk-goo^k]* is a beef seaweed soup that is associated with certain superstitions. Koreans don't eat it on the eve of an important day – for example, an exam or an interview – because they believe that the slippery nature of the seaweed may make the opportunity harder to grab.
- 삼계탕 **samgyetang** *[sam-gyay-tang]* *ginseng chicken soup* is actually a whole chicken stuffed with rice and spices and served in hot broth. It is traditionally eaten in the summer and is believed to be very good for the health.

On the menu

Let's look at some of the terms you might see on a typical Korean 메뉴 **menyu** *menu*. The key ingredient will be followed by the way it is prepared.

fritter / tempura	튀김 **twigim**	*twee-geem*
grilled	구이 **gui**	*koo-ee*
noodles	면 **myeon**	*myawn*
pancake	부침개 **buchimgae /** 전 **jeon**	*poo-chim-geh / chawn*
steamed	찜 **jjim**	*cHim*
stirfried	볶음 **bokkeum**	*poK-uhm*

Traditional Korean foods are prepared using methods other than an oven (grilled, deep-fried, panfried, steamed, etc.):

How is it cooked?
어떻게 요리해요?
eotteoke yorihaeyo?
aw-Taw-kay yo-ree-heh-yo
how cook

It is deep-fried.
튀김을 튀겨요.
twigimeul twigyeoyo.
tee-geem-uhl tee-gaw-yo
fritter fry

The vegetables are stirfried.
야채를 볶아요. **yachaereul bokkayo.**
ya-cheh-ruhl poK-a-yo
vegetable stirfry

The fish is grilled.
생선을 구워요.
saengseoneul guwoyo.
seng-sawn-uhl koo-wo-yo
fish grill

The noodles are boiled.
국수를 삶아요.
guksureul salmayo.
kook-soo-ruhl salm-a-yo
noodle boil

The dumplings are steamed.
만두를 쪄요.
mandureul jjyeoyo.
man-doo-ruhl cHaw-yo
dumpling steam

We make the gimbap.
김밥을 말아요.
gimbabeul marayo.
keem-bap-uhl mar-a-yo
gimbap roll

The kimchi stew is boiled.
김치찌개를 끓여요.
gimchijjigaereul kkeuryeoyo.
keem-chee-CHee-geh-rul Kuhr-aw-yo
kimchi-stew boil

The pancake is griddled.
전을 부쳐요.
jeoneul buchyeoyo.
chawn-uhl poo-chaw-yo
pancake griddle

If you want to ask what's in a dish:

What's in bibimbap?
비빔밥에 뭐가 들어있어요?
bibimbabe mwoga deureoisseoyo?
pee-bim-pab-ay mwo-ga tuhr-aw-eess-aw-yo
bibimbap-in what there-is

Note that there are two words for rice (uncooked and cooked):

rice (uncooked ~)	쌀 **ssal**	*ssal*
rice (cooked ~) / meal	밥 **bap**	*pa[p]*

side dish	반찬 **banchan**	*pan-chan*

The choice of desserts is rather limited, but there is often fruit such as pear, melon or persimmon or sweet rice cakes.

dessert	디저트 **dijeoteu /** 후식 **husik**	*tee-jaw-tuh / hoo-shi[k]*
fruit	과일 **gwail**	*kwa-il*
ice cream	아이스크림 **aiseukeurim**	*a-ee-s-k-reem*
ice cream topped with red bean paste	팥빙수 **patbingsu**	*pat-bing-soo*
rice cake	떡 **tteok**	*Taw[k]*

Seasonings and condiments

Korean condiments are largely based on various fermented foods: 간장 **ganjang** *soy sauce* is made from fermented soya beans, 고추장 **gochujang** is a mixture of fermented soya beans and red chili, 된장 **doenjang** is a fermented soya bean paste, and 액젓 **aekjeot** is fermented fish sauce.

What is it seasoned with?
무슨 양념을 사용해요? **museun yangnyeomeul sayonghaeyo?**
moo-sun yang-nyawm-uhl sa-yong-heh-yo
what seasoning use

fish sauce	액젓 **aekjeot**	*ek-jaw^{t}*
garlic	마늘 **maneul**	*ma-nuhl*
red chili paste	고추장 **gochujang**	*ko-choo-jang*
red chili powder	고추 가루 **gochu garu**	*ko-choo ga-roo*
salt	소금 **sogeum**	*so-guhm*
sesame oil	참기름 **chamgireum**	*cham-gee-ruhm*
soy sauce	간장 **ganjang**	*kan-jang*
soya bean paste	된장 **doenjang**	*tayn-jang*
sugar	설탕 **seoltang**	*sawl-tang*
vinegar	식초 **sikcho**	*shik-cho*

Talking about taste

Take note of the verb 맵다 **maepda** *to be spicy* as many Korean dishes can be hot!

It is ...		
bitter.	써 **sseo**	*saw*
a bit bland.	조금 싱거워 **jogeum singgeowo**	*cho-gum shing-gaw-wo*
delicious.	맛있어 **masisseo**	*mash-eess-aw*
greasy.	느끼해 **neukkihae**	*nuh-Kee-heh*
very salty.	많이 짜 **mani jja**	*man-ee CHA*
sour.	셔 **syeo**	*shaw*
spicy.	매워 **maewo**	*meh-wo*

sweet / sugary.	달아 **dara**	*tar-a*
sweet and sour.	새콤달콤해 **saekomdalkomhae**	*seh-kom-tal-kom-heh*
	...요. **yo.**	*yo*

Drinks

The most popular Korean alcohol (partly due to its low price!) is 소주 **soju** *[so-joo]*, which is a clear spirit traditionally made from rice, wheat or barley. Sometimes fruit or flavourings are added, so you can find 레몬소주 **remonsoju** *lemon soju*, 키위소주 **kiwisoju** *kiwi soju*, 인삼주 **insamju** *ginseng soju*, etc.

Another traditional Korean drink is 막걸리 **makgeolli**, a milky, unfiltered rice wine. It is low in alcohol (6–8%) and its taste is mild and slightly sweet.

alcohol	술 **sul**	*sool*
alcoholic beverages	주류 **juryu**	*choo-ryoo*
beer	맥주 **maekju**	*mek-choo*
cocktail	칵테일 **kakteil**	*kak-tay-il*
rice wine	막걸리 **makgeolli**	*mak-gawl-lee*
sake (Japanese liquor)	청주 **cheongju**	*chawng-joo*
soju mixed with beer	소맥 **somaek**	*so-meh*^{k}
vodka	보드카 **bodeuka**	*po-duh-ka*
whisky	위스키 **wiseuki**	*wee-s-kee*
wine	포도주 **podoju** / 와인 **wain**	*po-do-joo* / *wa-in*

To respect Korean drinking etiquette, a younger person should turn his or her head to the side to drink in front of an older person, and drinks should be given and received using both hands. 건배! **geonbae!** *[kawn-beh] Cheers!*

Other beverages

Coffee culture in Korea is quite recent, but today it is booming – you can find coffee shops easily in cities. The traditional beverage is tea, which comes in many forms. Apart from black and green teas, there are fruit, flower and herbal teas: 유자차 **yujacha** *lemon tea* (made from the Asian citrus fruit, yuzu), 보리차 **boricha** *barley tea*, 국화차 **gukwacha** *chrysanthemum tea* and 쌍화차 **ssanghwacha**, a fragrant, slightly bitter medicinal tea made from a variety of herbs and roots.

The water is lukewarm.
물이 미지근해요.
muri mijigeunhaeyo.
moor-ee mee-jeeg-uhn-heh-yo
water be-lukewarm

The green tea is very hot.
녹차가 뜨거워요.
nokchaga tteugeowoyo.
nok-cha-ga Tuh-gaw-wo-yo
green-tea be-very-hot

The coffee is hot.
커피가 따뜻해요.
keopiga ttatteutaeyo.
kaw-pee-ga Ta-Tuht-eh-yo

The orange juice is cool.
오렌지 주스가 시원해요.
orenji juseuga siwonhaeyo.
o-ren-jee joo-suh-ga shee-won-eh-yo

The soda is cold.
콜라가 차가워요.
kollaga chagawoyo.
kol-la-ga cha-ga-wo-yo

drink	음료수 **eumnyosu**	*um-nyo-soo*
coffee	커피 **keopi**	*kaw-pee*
fruit juice	주스 **juseu**	*choo-suh*
tea	차 **cha**	*cha*

Shopping

Shops and services

Shops are generally open every day until 10:00 p.m. You can also easily find 24-hour 편의점 **pyeonuijeom** *convenience stores* in cities. When addressing customers, different terms may be used. In an upmarket store, shop assistants use 손님 **sonnim** or 고객님 **gogaengnim** *guest*. In a smaller shop, kinship terms such as 'older sister' or 'aunt' are used to express warmth. To get someone's attention, call out 저기요! **jeogiyo!** *Please!*

Excuse me, how much is this?
언니, 이거 얼마예요?
eonni, igeo eolmayeyo?
awn-nee ee-gaw awl-ma-yay-yo
older-sister, this be-how-much
customer (f.) to shop assistant (f.)

That really suits you!
언니한테 잘 어울리네요!
eonnihante jal eoullineyo!
on-nee-an-tay chal aw-ool-lee-nay-o
older-sister-to well fit
shop assistant (f.) to customer (f.)

A useful term: 장을 보다 **jangeul boda** *to go shopping*.

Is there a market near here?
근처에 시장이 있어요? **geuncheoe sijangi isseoyo?**
kuhn-chaw-ay shi-jang-ee eess-aw-yo
proximity-at market there-is

Where are the baskets?
장바구니가 어디에 있어요? **jangbaguniga eodie isseoyo?**
chang-pa-goo-nee-ga aw-dee-ay eess-aw-yo
basket where there-is

convenience store	편의점 **pyeonuijeom**	*pyaw-nee-jawm*
department store	백화점 **baekwajeom**	*peh-kwa-jawm*

duty-free shop	면세점 **myeonsejeom**	*myawn-say-jawm*
market	시장 **sijang**	*shi-jang*
shop assistant	점원 **jeomwon**	*chawm-won*
shopping centre	쇼핑센터 **syopingsenteo**	*sho-ping-sen-taw*
shopping trolley/cart	쇼핑 카트 **syoping kateu**	*sho-ping ka-tuh*
street vendor	노점상 **nojeomsang**	*no-jawm-sang*
superstore	대형마트 **daehyeongmateu**	*teh-hawng-ma-tuh*

The American system is used for storeys, so the ground floor is the 1st floor, the next floor is the 2nd floor, and so on.

Which floor is the stationery department on?
문구매장이 몇 층에 있어요?
mungumaejangi myeot cheunge isseoyo?
moon-goo-meh-jang-ee myaw[t] chung-ay eess-aw-yo
stationery-department what floor is-located

It's expensive.
비싸네요. **bissaneyo.**
pee-ssa-nay-yo

It's cheap.
싸네요. **ssaneyo.**
ssa-nay-yo

checkout / till	계산대 **gyesandae**	*kay-san-deh*
delivery	배송 **baesong**	*peh-song*
information desk	안내 **annae**	*an-neh*
sale / discount	세일 **seil** / 할인 **harin**	*say-il / har-een*

Books, newspapers, magazines and music

In Seoul, you will find large bookstores that sell not just books, but also magazines, music, films, etc. If you're looking for an *English-language newspaper*, ask for a 영자신문 **yeongjasinmun**.

Do you also sell comics?
만화책도 파나요? **manhwachaekdo panayo?**
man-ha-chek-doh pa-na-yo
comic-also sell

Where is the magazine section?
잡지 코너가 어디예요? **japji koneoga eodiyeyo?**
chap-jee ko-naw-ga aw-dee-yay-yo
magazine section where-be

book	책 **chaek**	*che[k]*
bookstore	서점 **seojeom**	*saw-jawm*
CD	**CD**	*see-dee*
dictionary	사전 **sajeon**	*sa-jawn*
DVD	**DVD**	*dee-vee-dee*
K-pop	케이팝 **keipap**	*kay-ee-pap*
music	음악 **eumak**	*uhm-a[k]*
music (pop ~)	팝송 **papsong**	*pap-song*
novel	소설책 **soseolchaek**	*so-sawl-che[k]*
poem collection	시집 **sijip**	*shee-jip*

Laundry and dry cleaning

Laundrettes, dry cleaners and alteration services are usually found in shopping malls. Shoe repair stalls are often found near bus stops and metro stations. To ask how long it will take, use the verb 걸리다 **geollida** *to take (time)*:
얼마나 걸려요? **eolmana geollyeoyo?** *How long will it take?*

Where is there an alterations/repair service?
수선실이 어디 있어요? **suseonsiri eodi isseoyo?**
soo-sawn-sheer-ee aw-dee eess-aw-yo

When can I come pick it up?
언제 찾으러 올까요? **eonje chajeureo olkkayo?**
awn-jay chaj-uh-raw ol-κa-yo
when pick-up come

Can you change the heel of this shoe, please?
굽 좀 갈아 주세요. **gup jom gara juseyo.**
koo^p jom kar-a joo-say-yo
heel please change please

laundry / dry cleaner	세탁소 **setakso**	*say-tak-so*
shoe repair	구두 수선 **gudu suseon**	*koo-doo soo-sawn*

Shopping for clothes

Korean traditional dress (한복 **hanbok**) is still worn for festivals and formal celebrations. If you're trying on clothes and want to make a comment about the item, use ㄴ **-n** / 은 **-eun** 것 같아요 **geot gatayo** *it seems to me that ...* after the adjective:
작은 것 같아요 **jageun geot gatayo** *it seems small to me*
큰 것 같아요 **keun geot gatayo** *it seems big to me*.

I like this garment.
이 옷이 마음에 들어요.
i osi maeume deureoyo.
ee osh-ee ma-uhm-ay tuhr-aw-yo
this garment like

What material is it made of?
무슨 재질이에요?
museun jaejirieyo?
moo-sun cheh-jeer-ee-ay-yo
what material-be

Can I try it on? (clothes)
입어 봐도 돼요?
ibeo bwado dwaeyo?
eeb-aw pa-doh teh-yo
put-on look can

Can I try them on? (shoes)
신어 봐도 돼요?
sineo bwado dwaeyo?
shin-aw pa-doh teh-yo
wear look can

Do you have it in another size?
다른 사이즈 없어요? **dareun saijeu eopseoyo?**
ta-ruhn sa-ee-juh awps-aw-yo
other size there-is-not

Where is the fitting/dressing room?
탈의실이 어디예요? **taruisiri eodiyeyo?**
tar-ee-shir-ee aw-dee-yay-yo
fitting-room where-be

Here are some terms for clothing and accessories:

accessories	액세서리 **aekseseori**	*ek-say-saw-ree*
bag	가방 **gabang**	*ka-bang*
dress	원피스 **wonpiseu**	*won-pee-suh*
hat	모자 **moja**	*mo-ja*
jeans	청바지 **cheongbaji**	*chawng-ba-jee*
pyjamas	파자마 **pajama** / 잠옷 **jamot**	*pa-ja-ma* / *cham-o[t]*
shirt	셔츠 **syeocheu**	*shyaw-chuh*
shorts	반바지 **banbaji**	*pan-ba-jee*
skirt	치마 **chima**	*chee-ma*
socks	양말 **yangmal**	*yang-mal*
stockings / tights	스타킹 **seutaking**	*s-ta-king*
suit	양복 **yangbok** / 정장 **jeongjang**	*yang-bo[k]* / *chawng-jang*
sweater / jumper	스웨터 **seuweteo**	*suh-way-taw*
swimsuit	수영복 **suyeongbok**	*soo-yawng-bo[k]*
T-shirt	티셔츠 **tisyeocheu**	*tee-shaw-chuh*
trousers	바지 **baji**	*pa-jee*
underwear	속옷 **sogot**	*sog-o[t]*

Shoes

shoes	신발 **sinbal**	*shin-bal*
boots / ankle boots	부츠 **bucheu**	*poo-chuh*
dress shoes	구두 **gudu**	*koo-doo*
dress shoes (women's ~)	여성 구두 **yeoseong gudu**	*yaw-sawng koo-doo*
loafers / slip-ons	단화 **danhwa**	*tan-ha*
sandals	샌들 **saendeul**	*sen-duhl*
slippers	실내화 **sillaehwa /** 슬리퍼 **seullipeo**	*shil-leh-ha / suhl-lee-paw*
tennis shoes / trainers	운동화 **undonghwa**	*oon-dong-ha*

Colours

black	검정 **geomjeong**	*kawm-jawng*
blue	파란 **paran**	*pa-ran*
green	초록 **chorok**	*cho-rok*
pink	분홍 **bunhong**	*poon-ong*
purple	보라 **bora**	*po-ra*
red	빨간 **ppalgan**	*ᴘal-gan*
yellow	노란 **noran**	*no-ran*
white	흰 **huin**	*heen*
... colour	...색 **saek**	*se[k]*

Smoking

Note that smoking is banned in all public places, including station exits, bus stops and parks. If you smoke in a non-smoking area (look out for the signs) or throw your butt on the ground, expect a fine! It is polite to ask first before lighting up.

Is this a 'No smoking' area? ('no-smoking area-be')
금연 구역인가요? **geumyeon guyeogingayo?**
kuhm-yawn koo-yawg-een-ga-yo

Do you mind if I smoke?
담배 펴도 돼요?
dambae pyeodo dwaeyo?
tam-beh pyaw-do teh-yo
cigarette smoke can

I'm a smoker.
담배를 피워요.
dambaereul piwoyo.
tam-beh-ruhl pee-wo-yo
cigarette smoke

Where can I put the butt?
담배꽁초를 어디에 버려요?
dambaekkongchoreul eodie beoryeoyo?
tam-beh-kong-cho-rul aw-dee-ay paw-raw-o
butt where-at throw

ashtray	재떨이 **jaetteori**	*cheh-tawr-ee*
fine	벌금 **beolgeum**	*pawl-guhm*
lighter	라이터 **raiteo**	*la-ee-taw*
non-smoker	비흡연자 **biheubyeonja**	*pee-uhb-yawn-ja*
smoker	흡연자 **heubyeonja**	*huhb-yawn-ja*
smoking area	흡연구역 **heubyeonguyeok**	*huhb-yawn-koo-yaw*[k]

Photos

Try out a photo booth, where you can choose effects to add to your photos and use them as stickers! The verb 찍다 **jjikda** *to shoot, to film* is used for taking pictures:
사진을 찍어요 **sajineul jjigeoyo** *I* (*you*, etc.) *take pictures*.

Could you take a photo of me?
사진 좀 찍어 주세요.
sajin jom jjigeo juseyo.
sa-jin jom chig-aw joo-say-yo
photo just take please

Press here.
여기를 누르세요.
yeogireul nureuseyo.
yaw-kee-ruhl noo-ruh-say-yo
here press

Can I take a photo of this?
이거 사진 찍어도 돼요?
igeo sajin jjigeodo dwaeyo?
ee-gaw sa-jin CHig-aw-doh teh-yo
this photo take can

I need to take an ID photo.
증명사진을 찍고 싶은데요.
jeungmyeongsajineul jjikgo sipeundeyo.
chung-myawng-sa-jin-uhl CHik-gaw ship-uhn-day-yo

Can you develop this film, please?
현상해 주세요. **hyeonsanghae juseyo.**
hyawn-sang-eh joo-say-yo

battery	배터리 **baeteori /** 건전지 **geonjeonji**	*peh-taw-ree / kawn-jawn-jee*
camera	카메라 **kamera /** 사진기 **sajingi**	*ka-may-ra / sa-jin-gee*
camera (digital ~)	디지털 카메라 **dijiteol kamera**	*dee-jee-tawl ka-may-ra*
colour / black & white photo	컬러 **keolleo /** 흑백 **heukbaek** 사진 **sajin**	*kawl-law sa-jin / huk-bek sa-jin*
film	필름 **pilleum**	*peel-luhm*
memory card	메모리 카드 **memori kadeu**	*may-mo-ree ka-duh*
sticker photo	스티커 사진 **seutikeo sajin**	*s-tee-kaw sa-jin*
sticker photo booth	스티커 사진기 **seutikeo sajingi**	*s-tee-kaw sa-jin-kee*

Souvenirs

You can find traditional crafts such as 한지 **hanji** (handmade paper) and embroidery as well as modern souvenirs in all tourist areas. In markets and some small shops you can try to bargain (가격을 흥정하다 **gagyeogeul heungjeonghada** *negotiate the price*). The more you buy, the better the discount!

How much is a fan?
부채 한 개에 얼마예요?
buchae han gaee eolmayeyo?
poo-cheh han geh-ay awl-ma-yay-yo
fan one unit how-much-be

2000 won.
2,000원이에요.
icheon wonieyo.
ee-chawn won-ee-ay-yo
two-thousand won-be

alcohol (traditional ~)	전통주 **jeontongju**	*chawn-tong-joo*
ballpoint pen	볼펜 **bolpen**	*pohl-pen*
bookmark	책갈피 **chaekgalpi**	*chek-gal-pee*
cosmetics / makeup	화장품 **hwajangpum**	*hwa-jang-poom*
doll	인형 **inhyeong**	*een-hyawng*
gift	선물 **seonmul**	*sawn-muhl*
key ring	열쇠고리 **yeolsoegori**	*yawl-say-ko-ree*
picture / painting	그림 **geurim**	*kuh-reem*
postcard	우편 엽서 **upyeon yeopseo**	*oo-pyawn yawp-saw*
souvenir	기념품 **ginyeompum**	*kee-nyawm-poom*

Business meetings

In professional contexts, keep in mind that punctuality is a measure of trust. Companies tend to be very hierarchical. To show respect in the workplace, as a general rule, people use the polite formal ending ㅂ **-m** / 습니다 **-seumnida**.

Making an appointment

When addressing or talking about someone in a professional context, add 님 **-nim** *sir, madam* after the title (or after the surname + title if you know the person well): e.g. 사장 **sajang** *president, boss* becomes 사장님 **sajangnim** *Mr/Ms President*. But don't use it if talking about yourself.

I am A of company B.
B 회사의 A입니다.
B hoesaui A imnida.
P hway-sa-ee A eem-nee-da
B company-of A-be

I'd like to make an appointment with the director.
사장님을 만나뵙고 싶습니다.
sajangnimeul mannaboepgo sipseumnida.
sa-jang-neem-uhl man-na-bep-ko ship-suhm-nee-da
president meet would-like-to

When could I meet with you/him/her?
언제 만나 뵐 수 있을까요?
eonje manna boel su isseulkkayo?
awn-jay man-na bel soo eess-uhl-ка-yo
when meet can

Would 11:00 a.m. be convenient?
오전 11시 괜찮으십니까?
ojeon yeol hansi gwaenchaneusimnikka?
o-jawn yawl han-shi ken-chan-uh-shim-nee-ка
morning 11 hour okay

Thank you very much.
감사합니다.
gamsahamnida.
kam-sa-ham-nee-da

I'm punctual. ('time well keep')
시간을 잘 지킵니다.
siganeul jal jikimnida.
shi-gan-uhl chal chi-kim-nee-da

When you arrive at the company, don't forget to use the honorific **-nim** after the name or title of the person.

May I help you?
어떻게 오셨습니까?
eotteoke osyeotseumnikka?
aw-ᴛaw-kay o-shaw[t]-suhm-nee-ᴋa
how come

I have an appointment with President Kim at 10 a.m.
10시에 김 사장님하고 약속이 있습니다.
yeol sie gim sajangnimhago yaksogi itseumnida.
yawl shi-ay keem sa-jang-neem-ha-go yak-sok-ee ee[t]-suhm-nee-da
10 hour-at Kim president-sir-with appointment have

Please wait a moment.
잠시만 기다려 주십시오.
jamsiman gidaryeo jusipsio.
cham-shee-man kee-da-raw joo-ship-shi-o
a-moment wait [polite softener]

I will show you to President Kim's office.
김 사장님께 안내해 드리겠습니다.
gim sajangnimkke annaehae deurigetseumnida.
keem sa-jang-neem-ᴋay an-neh-heh tuh-ree-gay[t]-suhm-nee-da
Kim president-sir-to lead allow-me

Business vocabulary

Here are some terms to help you get by in business contexts.

agreement	합의 **habui**	*hab-ee*
appointment	약속 **yaksok**	*yak-so[k]*

business / trade	사업 **saeop**	*sa-aw^p*
business (small ~)	중소기업 **jungsogieop**	*chung-so-kee-aw^p*
company	회사 **hoesa**	*hweh-sa*
conglomerate	대기업 **daegieop**	*teh-kee-aw^p*
cooperation / collaboration	협력 **hyeomnyeok**	*hawm-nyaw^k*
development	개발 **gaebal**	*keh-bal*
distribution	배급 **baegeup**	*peh-guh^p*
export	수출 **suchul**	*soo-chool*
factory	공장 **gongjang**	*kong-jang*
import	수입 **suip**	*soo-ee^p*
investment	투자 **tuja**	*too-ja*
know-how / expertise	노하우 **nohau**	*no-ha-oo*
laboratory	연구실 **yeongusil**	*yawn-goo-shil*
management	경영 **gyeongyeong**	*kyawng-yawng*
marketing	마케팅 **maketing**	*ma-kay-ting*
meeting	미팅 **miting**	*mee-ting*
partner	파트너 **pateuneo**	*pa-tuh-naw*
quality	품질 **pumjil**	*poom-jil*
quantity	수량 **suryang**	*soo-ryang*
sub-contractor	하청업체 **hacheongeopche**	*ha-chawng-aw^p-chay*
turnover	매출 **maechul**	*meh-chool*

Let's sign the contract.
계약서에 싸인합시다. **gyeyakseoe ssainhapsida.**
kay-yak-saw-ay ssa-een-ap-sh-da
contract-on sign

modification of contract	계약 변경 **gyeyak byeongyeong**	*kay-ya^k pawn-gyawng*
cancellation of contract	계약 취소 **gyeyak chwiso**	*kay-ya^k chee-so*

Fairs and trade shows

Korea hosts a number of major international trade fairs: for example, at the COEX Convention & Exhibition Center in Seoul.

expo / trade fair	박람회 **bangnamhoe**	*pang-nam-hay*
exhibition centre	전시장 **jeonsijang**	*chawn-shi-jang*
sample	견본 **gyeonbon**	*kyawn-bon*

↗ Health

If you need medical attention ...

Korea has a high-quality, affordable public health care system. There are practitioners of both Western medicine and 한의학 **hanuihak** *[han-ee-a^k]* *traditional Korean medicine* (which includes herbal remedies and acupuncture, among other treatments). Both medical traditions are widely available. The country has also become the world capital of cosmetic surgery, leading to a boom in medical tourism. Like anywhere, it is normally necessary to make an appointment to see a doctor in Korea–then you will need to fill out a form at reception when you arrive.

Have you registered?
접수하셨어요?
jeopsuhasyeosseoyo?
chawp-soo-ha-shawss-aw-yo
registration-do

A&E / ER	응급실 **eunggeupsil**	*ung-guhp-shil*
blood type/group	혈액형 **hyeoraekyeong**	*hyawr-ek-yawng*
cosmetic surgery	성형수술 **seonghyeongsusul**	*sawng-hyawng-soo-sool*

dermatology	피부과 **pibugwa**	*pee-boo-kwa*
doctor	의사 **uisa**	*wee-sa*
intensive care unit	중환자실 **junghwanjasil**	*choong-hwan-ja-shil*
medical history	병력 **byeongnyeok**	*pyawng-nyaw^k*
medical insurance card	의료보험증 **uiryoboheomjeung**	*wee-ryo-po-hawm-chung*
medical treatment	진료 **jillyo**	*chil-lyo*
nurse	간호사 **ganhosa**	*kan-o-sa*
pediatrics	소아과 **soagwa**	*so-a-kwa*

Symptoms & ailments

If you need to describe your symptoms (증상 **jeungsang**):

I'm bleeding.
피가 나요.
piga nayo.
pee-ga na-yo
blood come-out

It itches.
간지러워요.
ganjireowoyo.
kan-ji-raw-wo-yo
tickling

I have a cough.
기침이 나요.
gichimi nayo.
kee-chim-ee na-yo
cough occur

I feel nauseous.
토할 것 같아요.
tohal geot gatayo.
to-al kaw^t kat-a-yo
vomit thing think

My legs are swollen.
다리가 부었어요.
dariga bueosseoyo.
ta-ree-ga poo-awss-aw-yo
leg swell

I can't see very well.
잘 안 보여요.
jal an boyeoyo.
chal an bo-yaw-yo
well not see

I hurt my arm.
팔을 다쳤어요.
pareul dachyeosseoyo.
par-uhl ta-chawss-aw-yo
arm injure

My wrist feels numb.
손목에 감각이 없어요.
sonmoge gamgagi eopseoyo.
son-mog-ay kam-gag-ee awps-aw-o
wrist feeling there-is-not

I'm constipated.
변비에 걸렸어요.
byeonbie geollyeosseoyo.
pyawn-bee-ay kawl-lawss-aw-yo
constipation have

I'm tired all the time.
항상 피곤해요.
hangsang pigonhaeyo.
hang-sang pee-gon-eh-yo
always tired

I ...		
have diarrhoea.	설사를 해 **seolsareul hae**	*sawl-sa-ruhl heh*
have a fever.	열이 나 **yeori na**	*yawr-ee na*
have indigestion.	소화가 안 돼 **sohwaga an dwae**	*so-wa-ga an deh*
have palpitations.	심장이 두근거려 **simjangi dugeungeoryeo**	*shim-jang-ee too-guhn-gaw-raw*
am having trouble breathing.	숨 쉬기가 힘들어 **sum swigiga himdeureo**	*soom shee-kee-ga heem-duhr-aw*
feel cold.	추워 **chuwo**	*choo-wo*
feel dizzy.	어지러워 **eojireowo**	*aw-jee-raw-wo*
	...요. **yo.**	*yo*

AIDS	에이즈 **eijeu**	*ay-ee-juh*
cancer	암 **am**	*am*

I'm paralyzed.
마비됐어요.
mabidwaesseoyo.
ma-bee-dehss-aw-yo

Pains and body parts

To say where the pain or problem is, the construction is body part + 아파요 **apayo** *ache, hurt, feel unwell* (the polite informal present of the verb 아프다 **apeuda** *to ache, to hurt, to be ill*).

I have a stomachache. ('stomach-[subject] hurt')
배가 아파요.
baega apayo.
peh-ga a-pa-yo

ankle	발목 **balmok**	*pal-mo^k*
arm	팔 **pal**	*pal*
back	등 **deung**	*tuhng*
bladder	방광 **banggwang**	*pang-gwang*
ear	귀 **gwi**	*kee*
eye	눈 **nun**	*noon*
foot	발 **bal**	*pal*
hand	손 **son**	*sohn*
head	머리 **meori**	*maw-ree*
heart	심장 **simjang**	*shim-jang*
hip	둔부 **dunbu**	*toon-boo*
intestine	장 **jang**	*chang*
knee	무릎 **mureup**	*moo-ruh^p*
leg	다리 **dari**	*ta-ree*
liver	간 **gan**	*kan*
mouth	입 **ip**	*ee^p*
nose	코 **ko**	*ko*
shoulder	어깨 **eokkae**	*aw-ᴋeh*
stomach / abdomen	위 **wi** / 배 **bae**	*wee / peh*
testicle	고환 **gohwan**	*ko-han*
throat	목 **mok**	*mo^k*
waist / lower back	허리 **heori**	*haw-ree*

Women's health

If you prefer to be treated by a female doctor, you can ask: 여의사를 불러 주세요. **yeouisareul bulleo juseyo.** *Can you call a female doctor, please?* ('woman-doctor call please').

I take the pill.
피임약을 복용해요.
piimyageul bogyonghaeyo.
pee-eem-yag-uhl pog-yong-eh-yo
pill take

I'm pregnant.
임신했어요.
imsinhaesseoyo.
eem-shin-ehss-aw-yo
be-pregnant

I have terrible cramps.
생리통이 심해요.
saengnitongi simhaeyo.
seng-nee-tong-ee shim-eh-yo
cramps be-severe

childbirth / labour	출산 **chulsan**	*chool-san*
condom	콘돔 **kondom**	*kon-dom*
gynaecologist / obstetrician	산부인과 의사 **sanbuingwa uisa**	*san-boo-in-kwa wee-sa*
miscarriage	유산 **yusan**	*yoo-san*
ovum / egg	난자 **nanja**	*nan-ja*
pregnant woman	임산부 **imsanbu**	*eem-san-boo*
sanitary towel / tampon	생리대 **saengnidae /** 탐폰 **tampon**	*seng-nee-deh / tam-pon*
sexual intercourse	성관계 **seonggwangye**	*sawng-gwan-gay*
sterility	불임 **burim**	*poor-eem*
uterus	자궁 **jagung**	*cha-goong*
vagina	질 **jil**	*chil*

Getting treatment

Western treatments are available, as are various forms of Korean traditional medicine such as 침술 **chimsul** *acupuncture.*

You need an operation.
수술해야 해요.
susulhaeya haeyo.
soo-sool-eh-ya heh-yo

We need to do an X-ray.
X레이 촬영을 해야 해요.
Xrei chwaryeongeul haeya haeyo.
Xray-ee chwar-awng-uhl heh-ya heh-yo

anaesthesia	마취 **machwi**	*ma-chee*
bandage / dressing	밴드 **baendeu**	*pen-duh*
blood pressure	혈압 **hyeorap**	*hyawr-a[p]*
blood test	혈액 검사 **hyeoraek geomsa**	*hyawr-eh[k] kawm-sa*
hospitalization	입원 **ibwon**	*eeb-on*
injection / shot	주사 **jusa**	*choo-sa*
operation	수술 **susul**	*soo-sool*
physical therapy	물리 치료 **mulli chiryo**	*mool-lee chi-ryo*
plaster cast	깁스 **gipseu**	*keep-suh*
pulse	맥박 **maekbak**	*mek-ba[k]*
stethoscope exam	청진 **cheongjin**	*chawng-jin*
temperature (body)	체온 **cheon**	*chay-on*
ultrasound	초음파 검사 **choeumpa geomsa**	*cho-uhm-pa kawm-sa*

At the dentist's

This back tooth hurts.
어금니가 아파요.
eogeumniga apayo.
aw-guhm-nee-ga a-pa-yo
molar hurt

You have a cavity.
충치가 있어요.
chungchiga isseoyo.
choong-chi-ga eess-aw-yo
cavity have

abscess / infection	종기 **jonggi**	*chong-gee*
braces	치아 교정기 **chia gyojeonggi**	*chee-a kyo-jawng-gee*
cleaning / scaling	스케일링 **seukeilling**	*s-kay-il-ling*
dentist (dentist's office)	치과 **chigwa**	*chee-gwa*
filling	아말감 **amalgam**	*a-mal-gam*
gums	잇몸 **inmom**	*een-mohm*
tooth	치아 **chia / 이 i**	*chee-a / ee*

At the optician's

I need a new pair of glasses / to repair my glasses.
안경을 맞추고 싶은데요 / 고치고 싶은데요.
angyeongeul matchugo sipeundeyo / gochigo sipeundeyo.
an-gyawng-uhl mat-choo-go ship-uhn-day-yo / ko-chee-go ship-uhn-day-yo
glasses make would-like-to / repair would-like-to

contact lenses	콘텍트 렌즈 **kontekteu renjeu**	*kon-tek-tuh ren-juh*
contact lenses (disposable ~)	일회용 렌즈 **ilhoeyong renjeu**	*il-ay-yong ren-juh*
contact lens solution	렌즈 용액 **renjeu yongaek**	*ren-juh yong-e*[k]
eye test (for vision)	시력검사 **siryeokgeomsa**	*shi-ryawk-kawm-sa*
eyeglass frames	안경테 **angyeongte**	*an-gyawng-tay*
eyeglass lenses	안경알 **angyeongal**	*an-gyawng-al*
optician	안경사 **angyeongsa**	*an-gyawng-sa*
left eye	왼쪽 눈 **oenjjok nun**	*wen-CHOK noon*
right eye	오른쪽 눈 **oreunjjok nun**	*o-ruhn-CHOK noon*

At the pharmacy

Note the verb 복용하다 **bogyonghada** *to take medicine*.

Apply this ointment.
연고를 바르세요.
yeongoreul bareuseyo.
yawn-go-ruhl pa-ruh-say-yo
ointment apply

Take this 3 times a day.
하루 3 번 복용하세요.
haru se beon bogyonghaseyo.
ha-roo say bawn pog-yong-ha-say-yo
day 3 times take

medicine	약 **yak**	*ya^k*
pharmacy	약국 **yakguk**	*yak-goo^k*
before a meal	식전 **sikjeon**	*shik-jawn*
after a meal	식후 **siku**	*shik-oo*
empty stomach	공복 **gongbok**	*kong-bo^k*

anti-nausea medicine	멀미약 **meolmiyak**	*mawl-mee-ya^k*
antiseptic / disinfectant	소독약 **sodongnyak**	*so-dong-nya^k*
baby products	유아용품 **yuayongpum**	*yoo-a-yong-poom*
cold medicine	감기약 **gamgiyak**	*kam-gee-ya^k*
diarrhoea medicine	설사약 **seolsayak**	*sawl-sa-ya^k*
feminine hygiene products	여성용품 **yeoseongyongpum**	*yaw-sawng-yong-poom*
fever reducer	해열제 **haeyeolje**	*heh-yawl-jay*
indigestion medicine	소화제 **sohwaje**	*so-wa-jay*
laxative	변비약 **byeonbiyak**	*pyawn-bee-ya^k*
pain reliever	진통제 **jintongje**	*chin-tong-jay*
prescription	처방전 **cheobangjeon**	*chaw-bang-jawn*
vitamins	비타민 **bitamin**	*pi-ta-min*

Index

Korean - Publication number: 3600
Printed in Slovenia
March 2017